The Effective Team's

Facilitation

By Elisabeth Goodman

RiverRhee Publishing

Published in the United Kingdom by RiverRhee Publishing, a trading name of RiverRhee Consulting Ltd, 49 Meldreth Road, Shepreth, Nr Royston, Herts SG8 6PS.

Copyright © Elisabeth Goodman 2018

All rights reserved. No portion of this book may be reproduced, stored in a retrieval system or transmitted at any time or by any means mechanical, electronic, photocopying, recording or otherwise, without prior written permission of the publisher.

The right of Elisabeth Goodman to be identified as the author of this work has been asserted by her in accordance with the Copyright, Designs and Patent Act, 1988.

A CIP record of this book is available from the British Library.

First printed in November 2018.

ISBN 978-0-9926323-9-7

Printed in Great Britain by Cambridge Printers Limited

Contents

Acknowledgements   i

Preface   ii

Introduction to the Practical Scenarios   iv

Chapter 1   Understanding the Brief   1
- What is facilitation?
- Understanding the client or sponsor
- Establishing rapport and trust with your client
- Clarifying the brief

Chapter 2   Taking care of the Logistics   9
- Venue space and layout
- Working across geographical locations and time zones
- Audio-visual requirements
- Refreshments
- Other bits and bobs of a facilitator's kit

Chapter 3   Managing the Participants   15
- Pre-work and joining instructions
- Break out groups and seating arrangements
- Ground rules and expectations
- Establishing your credibility, building rapport, dealing with emotions
- Wrap-up: action plans and feedback

Chapter 4   Selecting your Tools   25
- Basic good practices for facilitation
- Ice breakers
- Whole group presentations and discussions
- Break out groups for discussions and exercises
- Team building and development events
- Managing change
- Process improvement
- Knowledge management

Chapter 5   Managing Yourself   47
- Making the best use of your skillset
- Looking after your emotional wellbeing
- Looking after your physical wellbeing

Chapter 6   What Happens Next?   51

Materials for Use in Workshops   53

Fully Developed Practical Scenarios   57

Further Reading   63

Acknowledgements

My journey into facilitation, as with many of the topics for my "The Effective Team's" workbooks, began in the 1990s when I was working at SmithKline Beecham. It seemed that our Information Management department was often at the forefront of new ways of working and facilitation was another case in point.

The organisation had engaged Jill Fairbanks to provide training in facilitation, in what was to become the forerunner of "Simply Better Way": SmithKline Beecham's version of Total Quality Management (TQM) and what has since evolved into Lean and Six Sigma and other process improvement techniques.

I volunteered to be one of the first people to benefit from Jill's training, and so began my journey into a skill that fundamentally underpins my way of thinking and working with others.

Fellow facilitators that I have learned from include Ian Hau and Dan Law in my work on "Simply Better Way", and on Knowledge Management at SmithKline Beecham; Helen Chapman, Jackie Alexander and John Riddell in my work at GlaxoSmithKline (GSK) also on Knowledge Management; Sue Parkins, Nigel Clarke, Craig LeHoullier, Margie Gardiner, Gary Aldam also at GSK on Lean and Six Sigma.

I also worked with Helen after GSK as a co-facilitator for Pelican Coaching, whilst John and Margie have worked with me at RiverRhee Consulting. I have also learned so much from other past and current RiverRhee Associates: Lucy Loh, Janet Burton, Liz Mercer, John Hicks, Alison Proffitt and, more recently, Mark Strivens. I have even, in the last few months, had the pleasure to learn from a new partnership with Ludo Chapman at The Innovation Practice.

Other skillful facilitators that I have learnt from over the years include Chris Collison (author of "Learning to Fly"[1] – an excellent Knowledge Management publication), David Gurteen (also a Knowledge Management practitioner), and David Hall (of the Ideas Centre – for creativity and innovation practices).

Facilitation is a skill that I continue to practise and develop, as I work with fellow facilitators, with participants in events that I facilitate, and whenever I attend an event organised by others. Facilitation is a cornerstone of my work with managers and teams in Library and Information Management and in the Life Sciences. It underpins my approach for RiverRhee workshops, courses and even for one-to-one coaching sessions. And I have used it in voluntary work too, such as in the U3A French Conversation group, which I led for 3 years. (This led to another publication "Conversation s'il vous plait!"[2] under the RiverRhee Publishing label.)

This is the fifth and last of my workbooks for effective teams. My thanks go to Nathaniel Spain again for conceiving and creating the cover illustration, and for the other illustrations in this book. Jonathan Spain continues to be my greatest fan and enthusiastic co-author for the RiverRhee Publishing brand. Thank you.

Preface

Does the prospect of working with a room full of total strangers (or colleagues even) fill you with excitement? Do you get a glow of pleasure when you see people literally lighting up with a break-through in their thinking?

It was one such moment in an otherwise unremarkable and gloomy hotel meeting room somewhere in Philadelphia in the early 2000's that confirmed to me that I wanted to be a facilitator.

I get a buzz from creating situations where people can think differently about what they are doing, and come up with new perspectives and ideas that will help them to move forward. It does not have to be a major breakthrough. It could be some small incremental improvement, or just feeling happier and more in control of their work.

As a facilitator you are responsible for providing the setting, the atmosphere, the mood and the tools that will enable two or more people to productively think through whatever it is that they have set out to do. Put simply: facilitation is about providing people with the time and the space to think.

In order to do this effectively, you need to:

- Properly understand the client's brief and go beyond that to address what they might not have said or considered for themselves.
- Ensure that whoever is providing the room has included everything you asked for, whilst still expecting to have to improvise on the day for the un-anticipated omissions and quirks of the venue.
- Be prepared for whatever unpredictable emotions and dynamics might arise whenever a group of people gets together for the day.
- Be knowledgeable about and skillful with the tools that you bring to the workshop and how you use them to facilitate the content of the discussion.
- Manage your own energy, thinking and emotions throughout the day!

This book, "The Effective Team's Facilitation Workbook", the fifth and last in my series of workbooks for teams, is a celebration of all of the aspects I have learnt over the years to help me enjoy being a facilitator. I hope it will help others to do the same.

I am assuming that people reading the book will broadly fall into one of two categories. You will either be facilitating colleagues in your own team or organisation – the title of this book is geared to you! Or you may, like me, be facilitating teams or groups in other organisations – the book should work very well for you too.

The approach and format for the workbook is much like that of my previous four. It can act as a refresher for people who have attended one of my workshops relating to facilitation (a new offering planned for 2019), or where I have referenced some of the approaches. It can be used as a stand-alone manual for individuals who wish to learn about the different ways that they could facilitate groups and teams in their work. It can also provide the basis for planning and facilitating workshops with others.

Facilitation, perhaps more so than any of the other topics covered in my workbooks, is a discipline that improves with practice. It is a skill that you will add to and for which you will develop your own style. Please treat this book as an introduction if you are new to the discipline, or as a source of further tips if you are already experienced. Do get in touch if you would like me to help you further in your journey.

Each chapter of the book is designed to reflect my approach for running workshops on facilitation. The first chapter helps you to ensure that you understand the brief: who is your client (if it is not you) and what is the goal for the event you are facilitating? The chapters can be followed sequentially or dipped into to explore specific aspects of facilitation that you would like to learn about or improve upon.

There are practical scenarios to show how your approach to facilitation might vary according to different client situations and topics for an event. Each chapter has one or more exercises for reflecting upon or practising the principles and methodologies.

The workbook also includes support materials for some of the pre-work and an example of a feedback form that might be issued to participants for facilitated events.

The material on each of the three scenarios is also consolidated at the end of the book.

Finally, there are references for further reading for those who would like to find out more about various topics mentioned in this book.

Introduction to the Practical Scenarios

I will be using the following practical scenarios throughout the book to show how the various principles and methodologies can be applied. They are variations on the three that have I used in my previous books. They are partly based on real situations that I have encountered, but also adapted to better illustrate the points that I am making.

Scenario 1 – Running a centralised (shared) business service

A central library is picking up responsibility for core processes such as purchase of print and electronic resources, subscriptions and loans. It will support and be linked to a network of local libraries that interface with local business (or functional) groups. The head of the new central library has asked for two facilitated events:

- A workshop with representatives from the local libraries to prepare them for the change in responsibilities between the libraries, and to gain their input to shape the new processes that will be put in place.

A start up team building event for the new central library team.

Scenario 2 – Enhancing the effectiveness of scientific projects

A Life Science team is responsible for carrying out internal research projects, and study-related projects for external clients. It would like to carry out regular facilitated events to capture and share what the team has learnt and can learn from and share with others before, during and at the end of projects.

Scenario 3 - Refocusing the approach of an SME (Small or Medium Enterprise)

This organisation has significant opportunities to grow through the exploitation of internal and external knowledge and expertise. It has a number of different options for how to do this. A team development event is planned to begin to explore these options.

Chapter 1. Understanding the brief

"If we don't know what we are aiming for, we are unlikely to deliver it."

Figure 1. Understanding the client's brief

Background and principles

What is facilitation?

Facilitation, at its purest, is about providing the structure, processes and environment (both physical and emotional) for an event. Each of these aspects needs to be carefully selected and tuned to the nature of the sponsor or client* (whether internal or external), the intended outcome(s), the participants, and the constraints of the event.

(*I will be using the terms sponsor and client somewhat interchangeably.)

Where things can get fuzzy, is the extent to which the facilitator needs to get involved in the actual subject matter of the event. The general rule of thumb is not to get involved in participant specific content. But there are different levels of subject matter, which I will talk about here.

There will also be occasions when getting more involved in the content can be helpful and I will discuss this more fully in Chapter 4 on the tools for facilitation.

<u>The first level of subject content – the sector</u>
The sector is the area that the client comes from – so in my case that would be the Life Sciences, or Library and Information Management. If 'the client' is actually your own team or organisation, then you are likely to have this level of subject matter expertise.

Having a background in your clients' sector does help, because you feel that you are speaking the same language. You have an instant insight into the challenges and opportunities that your client may be facing. It helps to establish instant rapport and, with it, trust.

It is certainly possible to facilitate events for clients from a different sector to the one you are familiar with, but you might have to work harder at building the rapport and the trust.

Conversely, you have to consider how far to get involved in the detailed discussions around this kind of content: the day-to-day aspects of a client's work. This is what I will come back to in Chapter 4.

<u>The second level of subject content - the overall nature of the event</u>
Facilitators tend to specialise in certain disciplines that they can bring to an event. So for example my specialties are process improvement (Lean and Six Sigma), knowledge management, managing change, creating high performance teams. Other areas that I have helped to facilitate include business strategy, creativity and innovation.

Each of these disciplines will have a typical set of principles and tools that a skilled facilitator will gradually accumulate. I have referenced many of these in my previous workbooks, and will also reference some of them here.

This is the kind of content that your client is less likely to be familiar with, and for which they will be seeking your guidance.

However your client may want to develop knowledge and skills in this kind of content too. Certainly, one of my goals at RiverRhee is to build the client's capability in these disciplines so that they can gradually learn to facilitate future events themselves.

Individual or team reflection 1.1 Determining the subject content for events that you facilitate
What kind of event or events are you planning? Make some notes here:

- Are they for a particular sector? If so which?

- What area(s) of expertise will you (the facilitator) need to bring to the event or events?

- What knowledge or skills do you already have for this content? How will you address any gaps? What will you need to learn more about?

Cautionary note. If you are both the team leader and the facilitator for an event, you might want to think again about your approach. You may find it very difficult in practice to separate out how you want to contribute to the discussion from the objectivity required to ensure that the event runs smoothly and effectively. It may be better to recruit a facilitator from elsewhere in the organisation, or from outside.

Understanding the client or sponsor

The successful outcome of an event depends on everyone having a common understanding of the expectations.

This is true whether the event is an internal one for a team that you, as a facilitator, are used to working with; or whether you are facilitating an event for an external client.

Determining who the client is

Internal events bring their own challenges, as everyone may be assuming that they all have the same understanding of expected outcomes, when in fact this is seldom the case. So the first challenge here is working out who is the client or sponsor of the event. There may even be more than one.

The sponsor will be the one who will be evaluating the success of the event and making decisions on the basis of it. Who will you be reporting to about the event? Who will care? Is it just you?

If you are in fact the client or sponsor for an event, read the cautionary note under exercise 1.1 above.

The sponsor or client may not always be clear for **external events** that you are planning to facilitate. You need to find the decision maker: the one who will be relying on the outcomes and evaluating the effectiveness of the event.

Establishing rapport and trust with your client

There are a number of personality tools available to help you better understand yourself and others. I have referenced MBTI (Myers Briggs Type Indicator) and Belbin Team Roles for example in "The Effective Team's High Performance Workbook".

You would not expect to know other people's precise personality types from first impressions, or even from longer acquaintance. However, it is possible to pick up some general impressions of what's important to them and their general communication styles, using some essential everyday skills. These skills include the ability to ask good questions, to actively listen, and to pay attention to body language.

Exercising these everyday skills will not only help you to establish rapport and trust with your client, but also to engage with participants during events.

You can learn more about questioning, active listening and body language in Chapter 3. You could jump straight to that chapter to find out more, or you could just try a few things in this next exercise to help you better understand your client or sponsor.

Individual or team reflection 1.2 Understanding your client or sponsor

Who is the client or sponsor for your event? (If you don't know, how could you find out?)

What do you already know about what's important to your client or sponsor, and their communication style? *For instance are they very direct and not interested in "the fluffy stuff", or do they like to talk about feelings and emotions? Are they "big picture" thinkers or do they want to get into the detail of how things are going to happen?*

What questions could you ask, and how could you use your listening and observation skills to gain a greater understanding of your client or sponsor?

Clarifying the brief

It is essential to have clarity and agreement with your client about the desired outcomes from the event. There are some great questions you can ask to help with this:

- If this event were to deliver everything you wanted, what would that be? Or what would that look, sound, or feel like? (These are the kinds of questions an NLP (NeuroLinguisticProgramming) practitioner might ask.)
- What would you like to have happen? (This is a "Clean Language"[3] question.)

You may find that your client actually tells you this themselves, in which case your job will just be to replay what you have heard and to check that you have understood it correctly.

What often happens though is that the client only tells you some of what they are hoping to achieve from the event. Or they may dive straight into the approach that they have in mind. Or they may do some or none of these.

So the key thing is to let your client have his or her say, and then to begin asking the clarifying questions.

Once you have clarity about the desired outcome, you should also check for any other expectations and constraints that might have some impact on your approach. These expectations and constraints could include any one or more of the following:

- **The nature of the participants**: seniority and experience, organisational and reporting relationships, language skills, numbers
- **The nature of the venue**: location, size, layout and flexibility of layout – more about this in Chapter 2
- **Timing:** one day or two, half days, start and end times, anticipated date(s)
- **Materials:** any assumptions about what your or the client will be providing

Having gained a general understanding and agreement of the above, you can then begin to outline a possible approach. Again, the client may have given you a starting point for you to build from.

You will also need to agree how the brief and approach will be documented, and whether there will be one or more further discussions to finalise arrangements before the event itself.

Illustrations from the practical scenarios

Here is an example of how I might describe and write up the briefs for the practical scenarios, with the beginnings of the approach for the first of the three.

The approaches will be influenced by other factors that we will be exploring in the other chapters. The full approach for Scenario 1, and the approaches for the other two scenarios are therefore documented at the end of the book.

Scenario 1 – Running a centralised (shared) business service

Background and context

The central library is picking up responsibility for core processes such as purchase of print and electronic resources, subscriptions and loans. It will support and be linked to a network of local libraries that interface with local business (or functional) groups. The head of the new central library has asked for two facilitated events:

1. A workshop with representatives from the local libraries to:
   - Prepare the representatives for the change in responsibilities between the libraries
   - Agree the remits of the central and local libraries
   - Gain the representatives' input to shape the new processes that will be put in place.

This is to be a one-day event, led by the head of the central library, and attended by the team leaders of each of the five local libraries. It will be held in the main meeting room of the central library and facilitated by an external facilitator.

2. A start up team building event for the new central library team. This is to take place three months after the first workshop, once the members of the team have all been recruited. The purpose of this event will be:
   - To define the vision, mission, values of the group
   - To clarify roles, responsibilities and priorities for the next few months
   - To help the team understand its strengths and to start building strong relationships within the team. We have agreed that the MBTI (Myers Briggs Type Indicator) will provide the most useful insights for this team
   - To agree working practices for the team

This will also be a one-day event, led by the head of the central library. It is anticipated that there will be three additional team members. The event will also be held in the main meeting room of the central library and facilitated by an external facilitator.

The approach

Workshop 1 – an extract (the full approach is documented at the end of this book.)

Timing	Topic	Approach	Outcome
9:30 – 10:00	Welcome and introduction	Opening words from Head and Facilitator on goals and approach for the day. Introductions from team leaders on their expectations from the day.	Everyone aligned on goals, approach and expectations from the day.
10:00 – 11:00	Introducing the new remits	High-level overview of the new remits by Head – with Q&A. Facilitated exercise on perceptions of the change and what would help people to embrace it.	Everyone understands the overall intent going forward and has had an opportunity to air opinions and feelings relating to it. Head and individuals understand what they can do to help move forward positively with the change.

Scenario 2 – Enhancing the effectiveness of scientific projects

Background and context

The Life Science team is interested in regular facilitated events to capture and share what the team has learnt and can learn from and share with others before, during and at the end of projects.

As this implies a number of different styled events, the brief for the first one will therefore be as follows:

- To focus on an agreed recently completed project and use it as a model for how to conduct a learning review at the end of a project
- To agree how the team will share / address the learnings from the agreed project
- To explore how this approach could be extended to other projects, building in the approaches for learning before and during as well as at the end of projects
- To agree how the team will apply these approaches going forward

This is to be a one-day event, led by the team leader, and attended by all twenty-five members of the team. It will be held in a conference room on the research campus and facilitated by two external facilitators.

Scenario 3 - Refocusing the approach of an SME (Small or Medium Enterprise)

Background and context

The organisation would like to hold a team development event to explore options for exploiting internal and external knowledge and expertise.

The CEO would like to remind the organisation of the mission, vision and values of the organisation, and share their perspective of the opportunities available for exploring internal and external knowledge and expertise. She would like to then use the event to:

1. Enhance team members' understanding of the strengths that they can each bring to the organisation. We have agreed that the Belbin Team Roles will be particularly useful for this.
2. Have everyone contribute to a SWOT (Strengths, Weaknesses, Opportunities, Threats) analysis to share how well they think the organisation is currently exploiting internal and external knowledge and expertise.
3. Explore team members' ideas for what further activities they could undertake to better exploit internal and external knowledge and expertise.

This is to be a one-day event, led by the CEO, and attended by all thirty-five members of the team. It will be held in an external venue and facilitated by an external facilitator supported by an internal member of the organisation.

Individual or team reflection 1.3 Clarifying the brief for your next facilitated event

Think about the next event that you are planning.

What do you already know about the brief for this event?

What don't you know about the brief?

What questions would you like to ask?

How will you tackle that first discussion and subsequent discussions with your client? *For example what balance of listening vs. talking will you use? What will you try to cover in the first discussion? How will you document it? What will you return to in a second discussion?)*

Closing thoughts

A key point to remember when shaping the approach for a facilitated event is that you are the expert on how to do this. I have been in a couple of situations where events have not turned out as well as I or the client may have wished.

This has mainly been down to one of two reasons:

1. **Not being able to discuss the brief directly with the client.** The brief for an event has occasionally come through someone else. Although I have had some discussions with the client, they have been founded on expectations and assumptions made from earlier discussions that I have not been part of. The outcome as a result was not as good as it could have been.

So, a general rule is to either ensure you are part of any early discussion with a client or, if that's not possible, to effectively re-start the discussions from scratch.

You will need to clarify with the client that you are doing this, and why it is necessary to ensure that you fully understand their expectations.

2. **Not being direct enough with the client about the most effective approach.** Some clients can be quite assertive about the approach that they would like to take, and it can be quite difficult or uncomfortable to try to persuade them otherwise. This does not happen to me very often, but I have seen other facilitators struggle with this.

A possible way to deal with this situation is to have examples to hand of other events that you have facilitated: the approaches you used and what happened as a result.

Ideally, you would have examples to quote where the outcomes reflect the kind of results that your current client is after. If you have not got examples from events that you have facilitated, you might still have examples from events that you have otherwise witnessed.

Some final tips

Be prepared to retain some flexibility in your approach – after all there will surely be things that you can learn from your client!

Nor do you need to have all of your ideas at your fingertips for that first discussion with your client. You can treat that first discussion as a preliminary exploratory one, and then agree to come back to them with a more fully developed approach. That will give you a chance to do your research and homework on alternatives if you need to do so. You can always schedule a second discussion to talk through the alternatives.

Finally, think about what you can offer beyond the obvious to deliver real value to your client. So for instance, is there a model or tool you can illustrate; a relevant article you can give them; a printed poster or handout that they can retain for future reference? I will include examples of some of these in Chapter 4.

Chapter 2. Taking care of the logistics

"If people are comfortable, they are more likely to think productively!"

Figure 2.1 Logistical components of a venue

Background and principles

The importance of getting the venue right

It may seem strange to have a chapter on logistics so early in this book, but experience has taught me the importance of having this discussion with clients very early on. Problems will arise if it is left until too close to the event.

The flexibility of the venue will affect your choice of approach for the event, and your chosen approach may influence your requirements for the layout.

Most of my events are face-to-face, in one venue. So that is the type of situation I will focus on here. But I also have a sub-heading based on my experience of running events across more than one geographical location and time zone.

Every training course, workshop or team activity that I organise is based on reflection, discussion and interactive exercises. It is impossible to do these effectively in a confined meeting room, with only just enough space for people to sit around one large table.

One of my (and probably the delegates') most memorable negative experiences was of delivering a training course in a room with barely enough space to edge around the twelve delegates seated around the one square table. The corridor outside was a main thoroughfare so that there was the constant noise of a door banging as people went by. Whenever we wanted the delegates to have any kind of discussion, everyone would rush outside with great relief to find a bit of air, space and quiet to do so.

Another event I facilitated had the delegates sitting in small groups around tables where it was impossible for one person to stand up without asking at least two others to move. So it was very difficult to have people swap between different groups for different exercises as we had planned. We did just about manage it! Meanwhile, this constrained layout seriously inhibited our ability to check-in with people to ensure that they understood the exercises, and to address any issues or to offer suggestions. I, and my fellow facilitator, could only look on from afar and hope that people were managing – not an ideal situation at all.

It is not always possible to anticipate some of the peculiarities that you might encounter in the venue for your event. I had another venue that was beautifully spacious, but where the pictures on the walls were fixed in place, and pillars were dotted in awkward places, so that we could not easily put up flip chart pages to refer to through the day.

Knowing the importance of sufficient space for breakout discussions and exercises, wall space for flip charts, the ability to project slides, can at least help you to plan for these as well as possible. After that, all you can do is be prepared for the unexpected: turn up as early as is practical and be prepared to use your ingenuity and improvisation skills.

Venue space and layout

Off-site or on-site locations - how to choose?

Deciding whether to hold an event on- or off-site can be a simple matter of cost and availability. The choice may also be influenced by the participants' travel or home-life constraints.

Beyond that, it may be a matter of whether the client wants to create a special sense of occasion, or wants to ensure that participants do not get distracted by non-participating colleagues, or by their day job.

As a facilitator I would not insist too much on one or the other location, but would rather emphasize the importance of having a space that is fit for purpose, as described in the next sections.

Room space

I generally ask for a meeting room that is three times the size that would normally be allocated for the number of people involved. I do not always get that, but it does mean we are not usually squeezed in too tight.

The client may also offer some additional breakout space if they cannot provide a large enough main room. In that situation, it is important to ask for the breakout area or areas to be as close to the main room as possible. It can be very difficult to facilitate people spread across two or more rooms, unless you can get a second facilitator.

Wall space and surfaces

Most of the events that I organise involve breakout exercises where delegates record the discussion on flip chart pages, or on post-it notes which they then affix to flip charts. I also sometimes use pre-prepared posters. This visual approach is often an integral aid to the delegates' thinking. They will come back to the earlier flip charts as part of their reflection.

So having some way to attach flip chart pages and posters to the venue's walls is often integral to the success of the event. However, venues may not always have the space to do this (as with my earlier example of immovable pictures and pillars). Where they do have the space, they may have rules forbidding delegates to fix items on walls because of concern about the décor. Or they may only allow the use of certain means of adhesion: white tack instead of blue tack, or masking tape only. So this is another feature that it is important to check for in advance.

Some venues provide white boards, which, if plentiful enough, will work well. Others might, if requested, provide poster boards with drawing pins.

I also regularly use "Magic Chart": plastic sheets that adhere by static to almost any surface. I have been caught out though by highly varnished and patterned wood paneling, which the sheets did not stick to. Very vigorous air-conditioning can also prevent the sheets staying in place. These plastic sheets can be written on with white board pens, some of which will erase and so allow re-use.

Layout – tables and chairs

The ideal layout of the room will vary depending on numbers and on the nature of the event. We will be exploring the question of ratio of participants to facilitators in Chapter 3 in the context of optimizing engagement.

As a general rule, it works well to have a table at the front for whoever is leading the session and for the facilitator, and then a U-shape arrangement of tables and chairs for the participants.

A boardroom layout can work if there is enough space to move around the outside, work on flip charts on the walls and swap around for breakout discussions.

If there are more than six or seven delegates, then you might break them up into smaller groups, of between four to six people per group. This is referred to as cabaret or café style seating. Again, you will want to arrange the tables in such a way that people can easily see and interact with the leader of the session and with the facilitator, and to read anything that is being projected on a screen, or displayed on flip charts.

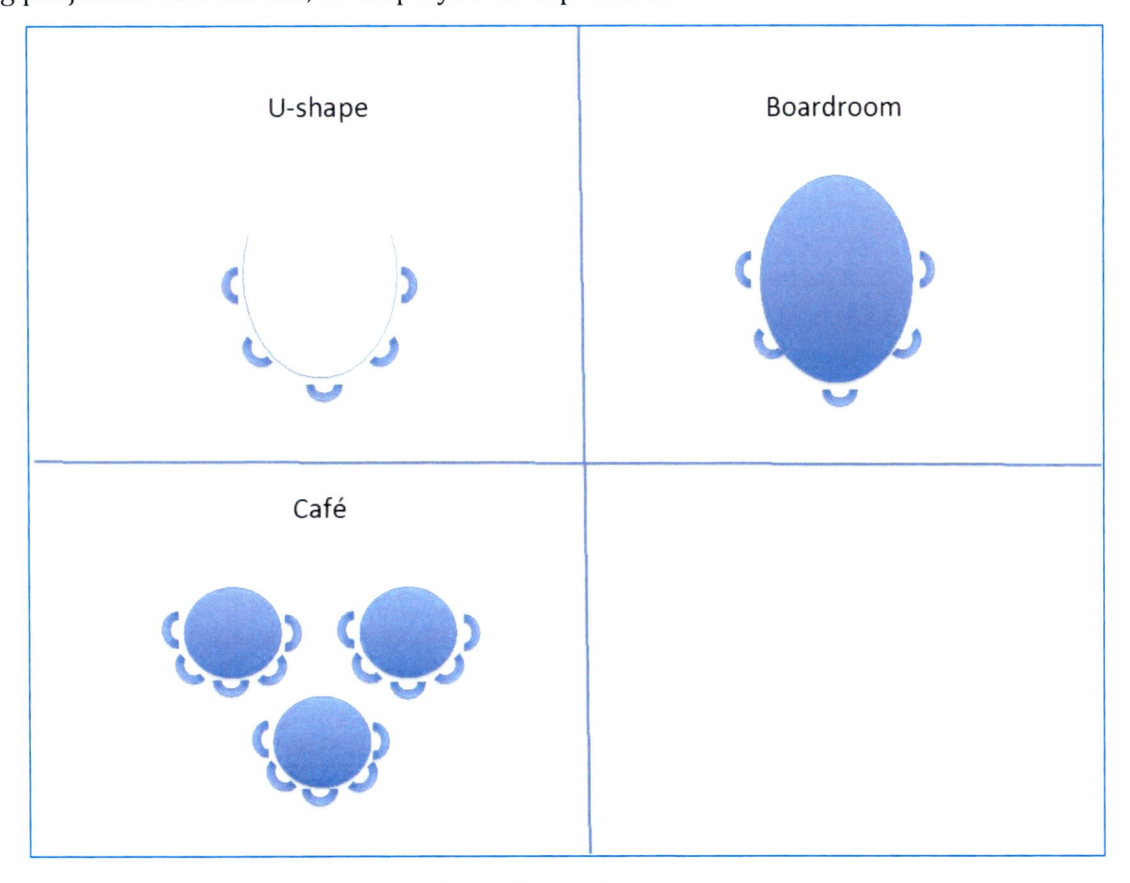

Figure 2.2 Sample seating arrangements

Some facilitators like to have delegates using chairs only, no tables. This may indeed be appropriate for certain types of events – for example where a high level of interaction and movement is involved. I have had some delegates tell me that only having a chair, with no table, can make them feel too vulnerable. Certainly, if there is any amount of course material, and any requirement for people to make notes, people will be a lot more comfortable with a table to lean on.

11

Working across geographical locations and time zones

I have occasionally facilitated events that span geographical locations and/or time zones and found it possible to work with some of the advantages of this form of communication.

If there are a number of people at each location, the key is to ensure that each one has its own facilitator, and to work with these additional facilitators as a team. Each location obviously needs to have suitable facilities, as described above for single face-to-face locations.

It can be a real advantage to have each location work on a portion of the content, and then to come together to share the result at periodic intervals. I have done this with UK / US (West Coast) meetings where the UK group has kicked things off in their morning; there was a joint 'handing-over' meeting in the UK afternoon / US morning. The US group then continued developing content in their afternoon ready for the UK to review the following morning.

Events where individuals are phoning in from different locations to participate in the main meeting taking place elsewhere can be harder to manage. Expectations should probably be set at the start as to how things will work, the level of participation and involvement that are likely to happen, and what the leader and facilitator of the event can do to optimise these.

Audio-visual requirements

It is fairly standard nowadays for meeting rooms to come equipped with a data projector, or with a TV screen. A laptop or computer might be provided in which to plug a memory stick. In most cases I have brought my own laptop, with the necessary VGA or HDMI adapters to plug into the client's cables.

If using HDMI and a TV screen, it is likely that the audio from any online videos will work effectively. It is a good idea to bring some form of plug-in loudspeaker as a backup. At any rate, these are the kinds of technology questions to check on in advance, and to test as soon as possible on arrival and ahead of the start of the event.

It can also be helpful to check that there will be a screen, or at least an appropriately placed blank wall to project onto, with the facility to dim the lights, or to block off natural light.

We have already discussed the use of flip charts, white boards, poster boards, "Magic Chart" above. A rule of thumb, if working with break out groups, is to ensure that there is something for each group to write on, as well as something at the front of the room for the leader and facilitator to use.

The final requirement, as mentioned when working across geographical locations, is suitable telecommunications to enable participation by remote participants.

Refreshments

If you are holding your event in-house your refreshments may be constrained by company policies and budgets. The same may be true for off-site venues, though the choice of refreshments is often greater there.

I have found that the most important provision to ensure there is plenty of is water! It is a proven fact that keeping hydrated helps our concentration and thinking powers. If the venue is air-conditioned then you will need even more water.

It is also a good idea to ensure that participants have access to tea and coffee on arrival, mid-morning, after lunch and mid-afternoon, and of course that there is lunch too for whole day events.

It is increasingly important to check on dietary requirements and provisions for those who do not drink caffeine, do not drink or eat dairy products, need gluten free, are vegetarian, vegans etc.

Beyond that, people are often enthusiastic about having pastries, cakes and biscuits – but watch out for the effects of sugar and carbohydrates as they can make people sleepy. So fresh and dried fruits and nuts are good alternatives or additions if you can get them.

Other bits and bobs of a facilitator's kit

It is worth getting yourself a strong box in which to keep materials that you might use on a regular basis.

My facilitator's kit includes the following:

- Blue tack, white tack, drawing pins, magnets and masking tape as alternatives for putting things up on walls.
- Sellotape, string and scissors for some of my more creative activities.
- "Post-it" notes of various colours, shapes and sizes.
- "Sharpie" pens, white board pens, flip chart pens.
- "Magic chart" rolls (these don't fit in the actual box)
- A collection of post-cards that I use for various activities

Some events require special materials for instance those covering such topics as:

- Belbin Team Roles – I have a set of specially made badges that I use, although there are also some available from the Belbin web site. Posters and other resources are also available.
- MBTI (Myers Briggs Type Indicator) – there are various books, posters and workshop materials available from the suppliers in the UK (The Myers-Briggs Company – formerly OPP.)

I also have various branded RiverRhee products:

- Writing pens and notepads that I use in venues that do not provide their own for delegates.
- A set of designs that I get printed as post-cards for delegates to record key actions at the end of some of my courses.
- A pull-up RiverRhee banner that I use for some events.

Individual or team exercise 2.1 Planning the logistics for your next event

What choice of venue and constraints do you have for the event that you are planning?

How many participants are you expecting?

What layout will work best for the numbers, the space you have available, and the types of activities you have planned? *(See also the closing thoughts.)*

What audiovisual equipment is available? What do you need to bring?

What flexibility do you have in terms of refreshments? Is there a budget?

What other materials do you want to ensure are available? What will you bring?

Closing thoughts

The layout you choose, and the materials you will need, will also depend on the nature of the event that you are facilitating. If it is an event on team building for one team there is likely to be a lot of very fluid interaction across the whole group.

If the event is on process improvement, with sub-groups working on their own processes, then the breakouts are likely to be more separated out.

It is likely that you will want to revisit your logistical requirements once you have worked through Chapter 4 and the various tools for facilitation.

Chapter 3. Managing the participants

"An individual's perception is reality."

Figure 3. Participants experiencing different emotions

Background and principles

A course, workshop or team event is only as successful as the perception it leaves in people's mind at the end of the day. The experience will be more or less positive depending on how well it meets or exceeds the expectations of the participants.

Will they learn something new, address an important challenge, advance their thinking, improve relationships with their colleagues and enjoy themselves?

These are the sorts of questions they may be asking themselves at the start of the event.

As a facilitator, your job is to provide an emotionally safe, positive and constructive environment as well as a structure to help these things happen. Ideally, whoever is leading the event will help you with this too!

We have already explored how to clarify the brief, and how to address the physical logistics for a productive event. This chapter covers other essentials for setting the scene, as well as strategies to use when things do not go quite according to plan.

Pre-work and joining instructions

We know that some people perform best if they know what will happen at an event, and if they have an opportunity to reflect on a topic in advance, rather than having to think on the spot.

Issuing delegates with pre-work will help some of them to be more productive, but it will also help to set expectations and build curiosity and commitment amongst all delegates.

It is a good idea to send 'joining' instructions with details of the goals of the event, where it is taking place, start and end-times, arrangements for lunch if applicable, and the agenda.

What pre-work is best will depend on the nature of the event, and how well you know the participants.

It is also your choice as to whether you ask participants to send you copies of their pre-work in advance, or to simply come prepared with it. My experience is that many participants are more likely to do the pre-work if you ask them to return it to you by a certain date!

In addition, you might use the pre-work as input for consolidating and presenting back during the event itself. Alternatively it can give you some very useful insights to help with your general preparation for the event.

Here are the kinds of things you might do for the different practical scenarios. (I have included examples of pre-work questionnaires in the workshop materials at the end of the book.)

Scenario 1 – Running a centralised (shared) business service

There are two events planned here:

1. The workshop with representatives from the local libraries with a focus on helping them to deal with the change, and on gaining their input for the new processes.
2. The start up team building event for the new central library team.

For the first workshop, whether you are an internal or an external facilitator, it would be a good idea to have a preliminary conversation with the head of the central library to gain their perspective on the members of the workshop and on how they are responding to the change. This will help you to be prepared for any potential sensitivity.

The exercises you plan on the day will help you to tease out feelings, emotions and attitudes further and hopefully respond to them in a constructive way.

You can help the delegates to come prepared with something that will help them to feel emotionally safe and positive by asking them to document the processes that the workshop will focus on. This documentation can take the form of flow-charts of current processes and/or initial thoughts on the 'to be' process. They can also document current good practices, as well as aspects of the processes that they know can be improved.

The second, team building, event has a number of components, as described in the brief in Chapter 1. Each of these could benefit from some specific pre-work, for example:

- *Defining the vision, mission, values of the group.* The pre-work here is essentially down to the head of the central library – with your support. The head can either come with some preliminary ideas that s/he can sound the rest of the team out about, or you can come with examples if the head would rather start with a clean sheet.
- *To clarify roles, responsibilities and priorities for the next few months.* Here you could ask participants to come with preliminary ideas about their roles to share and get reactions to during the event.
- *To help the team understand its strengths and to start building strong relationships within the team.* You will need to issue the MBTI questionnaire in advance of the event as this is the tool that client has agreed to use.
- *To agree working practices for the team.* You could ask delegates to reflect on the different working practices that are important to a high performance team (see full description in Chapter 4). Depending on how long they have been in the team, they could reflect on what is going well, and on what could be done to help the team and themselves be at their most productive.

Scenario 2 – Enhancing the effectiveness of scientific projects

The Life Science team event combines an actual learning review on an agreed project, with guidance and reflection on future learning practices before, during and at the end of projects.

The pre-work could therefore consist of a structured questionnaire on what worked well and what could have been done differently during the project. (See fuller descriptions of After Action Review and of Learning Reviews in Chapter 4.)

You could also ask them to reflect in advance on any existing good working practices for sharing learning before, during and after projects, and ideas for what could be done differently.

Scenario 3 – Refocusing the approach of an SME (Small or Medium Enterprise)

This organisation's team development event will be exploring a range of options for the exploitation of internal and external knowledge and expertise.

The brief includes the following elements:

1. Using Belbin Team Roles to enhance team members' understanding of the strengths that they can each bring to the organisation. You will need to issue the Belbin Team Roles questionnaire as pre-work.
2. A SWOT analysis and team members' ideas for what further activities they could undertake to better exploit internal and external knowledge and expertise. This could be set as pre-work for reflection and then discussion and consolidation during the event itself.

Break out groups and seating arrangements

In Chapter 2 we learnt about how the number of participants and the nature of the venue might constrain the choice of seating arrangements.

The third influence on breakout groups and seating arrangements is to do with the nature of the participants. There are a few aspects to this.

In an event for an intact team, or an intact organisation, there will be individuals reporting to each other. Obviously, if numbers are small (seven or less), you will have no choice but to keep everyone together.

For larger groups, you might want to consider alternatives.

Having participants sit with their managers could be important to consolidate their thinking. Separating them, on the other hand, could promote more independent thinking.

The same will be true if you have an event in which multiple teams are taking part. Mixing people across teams could lead to greater creativity, as well as the development of new networks.

I have facilitated events where I have mixed the members of breakout groups in the morning to stimulate more divergent thinking and networking, and then brought them back to their teams in the afternoon to consolidate or converge their thinking.

In events with intact organisations, where there is a senior management team taking part, and where the numbers allow, you might want to have one member of the management team sitting with each breakout group.

If there are no reporting relationships and the participants are more mixed, you might be happy to have them self-select their groups, or look for other areas of differences and similarities that might influence the groupings.

Either way, it is a good idea to ask your client for information in advance about the affiliation of the participants, and to discuss with him / her if any groupings would be a good idea.

Ground rules and expectations

Ground rules and expectations set the tone for the event and are all part of helping people to feel comfortable, safe and confident that their needs are being addressed.

Ground rules

When I attended internal or external events 20 or more years ago, they would always start with an agreement about ground rules. Sometimes the person starting the session would just put up a list. Other times they would ask the participants to suggest what should be on it.

Although agreeing ground rules seems less common now, I attended an external event recently where the facilitator did do that, and I found it a refreshing and reassuring start. So it is something you might want to consider.

The types of things that might appear in a set of ground rules include any of the following or more:

- Mobile phones off or on silent and out of sight and laptops closed
- Participants (and facilitator) respect timings
- Be present and attentive
- Listen to each other – no interruptions
- Give everyone equal air time (if they want it)
- Agree how to deal with tangential / off topic points as they arise (allow full discussion or 'park' them for later attention)
- Respect confidentiality

Expectations

Expectations come from the client, from you as the facilitator, and from the participants.

Your client's and your expectations are essentially the goals for the session: those that appeared in the brief. It is usual to share these in the joining instructions, and to reiterate them at the start of the event, often on a slide as well as verbally.

You might have asked the participants for their expectations as part of their pre-work. It is still useful to ask the participants to share their expectations verbally at the start of the session so that everyone is aware of them, and to demonstrate that each person's expectations has been heard.

For large groups I have written the expectations from the pre-work up on a flip chart in advance, and asked the participants to discuss them amongst themselves and let me know of any additions.

For smaller groups I have asked participants to verbalise their expectations with the whole room and written them up as they shared them.

In all cases I make it quite clear as the event proceeds that I am checking back on the expectations to make sure that they are being addressed. I also do a final review at the end of the event as part of the wrap-up (see below).

Establishing your credibility, building rapport, dealing with emotions

There is a whole emotional undercurrent to any occasion where people get together. The quality of this undercurrent determines the levels of trust and respect, and hence people's comfort with saying what they think and feel. It will also influence people's ability to think and learn.

The way you come across as a facilitator, your credibility and your ability to build rapport will all affect the emotions in the room.

Your credibility and building rapport

Some of us find it easier to talk about ourselves than others do! However I have found that, both as a facilitator and as a participant, some background really does help with establishing credibility and building rapport.

Some participants might assume that you have the necessary background and expertise to justify you being there. And they may be predisposed to trust you.

However, whether they acknowledge it to themselves or not, hearing just a short introduction from you as the facilitator about what you bring to the event and why you are there, will definitely help establish you as a knowledgeable, experienced and 'good to be with' person to spend a few hours or longer with.

Whether talking about yourself in this way is something that you are comfortable with or not, it is a good idea to think about what might be the most appropriate thing to say. Then practise it to help it come across as natural and comfortable.

I also find it helpful to talk to participants individually before the event kicks off. Doing this can help to 'break the ice' for the participants as well as for yourself and so make everyone feel more comfortable. It can also give you additional background information to help you tailor your approach or to reference in your introduction or during the event.

Emotions

Laughter amongst participants (of the right kind) is perhaps the most rewarding emotion to experience as a facilitator. Apparently, the intensity of the emotion associated with laughing makes for more memorable experiences.

Crying will also make an experience more memorable but that is likely to leave a negative impression.

And anger (without any immediate and positive resolution) is not to be advocated as that will create a barrier to learning for both the person expressing the anger, and the others witnessing it.

The worst kind of emotion for a facilitator to have to deal with though is apathy: when a participant is obviously not interested in what is going on.

Here are some reflections from my experiences of dealing with these different types of emotion.

Laughter

Enjoy it if it happens spontaneously – as long as it is well intentioned, and does not get in the way of quiet concentration. It can help if you are able to generate laughter through a well-positioned witticism, but keep it natural and do not try too hard. You need to maintain respect rather than trying to be 'one of them', and there is always the risk of making an inappropriate joke.

The 'wrong kind' of laughter – and something to be actively discouraged - is if it is at the expense of other participants and causes them discomfort. I have not experienced this. If it did happen I would probably find an opportunity to have a quiet word with the individual involved, or with my client if they were present.

Inside jokes that you are excluded from can feel uncomfortable for a facilitator but can be ignored – as I have done on the one occasion when I experienced this in an event.

Crying

I have had participants burst into tears (albeit quietly) on a couple of occasions.

Luckily, in the first case, I had another facilitator in the room. As the crying was continuing and obviously worrying both the individual and his neighbours, my co-facilitator offered the individual the chance to go outside with her. They had a short conversation during which the participant was given the option of staying out of the event or returning once he was composed. He did return and participated relatively comfortably for the rest of the session.

On the second occasion the individual took herself out of the room and returned shortly afterwards. It was apparent that she was taking measures to compose herself and that no intervention was needed on my part. A quiet word with her later confirmed that she had addressed the issue and was comfortable with continuing.

Conflict

We know, from the works of Dr Bruce Tuckman[4] and Daniel Goleman[5] that conflict can be a very positive thing. A dynamic to-ing and fro-ing of ideas and opinions will make for greater creativity and stronger relationships within a team. When people are expressing themselves with strength and conviction, the atmosphere can get very warm and there is a risk that it might tip into unproductive behaviour.

As a facilitator, you will need to judge how much to let the discussion flow, and when it might be necessary to intervene.

Behaviour could be considered as unproductive if people start attacking each other rather than their ideas and opinions; if the conversation becomes circular; if people leave the room. In these situations you would want to consider various options such as:

1. Pointing out what is going on
2. Summarising or asking people to summarise the different views being expressed
3. Encouraging people to hear each other out
4. Suggesting a break to allow emotions to cool down
5. Taking people to one side
6. Asking people to apologise

Lack of interest or engagement

This is perhaps one of the most frustrating situations to deal with as a facilitator. You want everyone to be engaged and enjoying themselves, but that will not always be the case.

You will need to exercise your judgment and not act too hastily. Some people might look like they are not engaged in the discussion, and yet they may simply be reflecting. Others may genuinely not want to be there.

Strategies I have used include:

- Observation and listening – give people time to settle in before you make any assumptions about their level of engagement.
- Direct an open question relating to the content of the event to the individual or individuals concerned: you will be able to tell by the way they answer whether they have simply been reflecting, or are really not engaged.
- Have a quiet word with the individual during a break-out exercise, or in a tea break to ask them what they think or feel about the event so far and how it might work better for them.
- If the individual's manager or the client is in the room, have a discussion with them to share your observation about the individual and discuss the approach the manager or client would like to take.
- On one occasion I have, with the agreement of the client, suggested to the individual that they leave the event. The individual concerned was happy to do so!

Wrap-up: action plans and feedback

The final step for creating a positive event is an effective closure or 'wrap-up'. The nature of the event will determine the specifics of what should be included in the wrap-up.

I have found that, as a rule, including a review of action plans, and some form of feedback against the original goals or expectations works particularly well.

Reviewing action plans

Reviewing the action plans individually and as a group, helps to build commitment.

For in-house events with intact teams or organisations, it demonstrates to the individuals that the time they have spent together and the contributions they have made is valued and will be followed-up.

Unfortunately, if you are an external facilitator, you have no guarantee that the actions will be progressed. It may be possible to agree a follow-up meeting with your client one to three months after the event to help with this.

For individuals at our events, there is something about writing their planned actions down, and perhaps even sharing them aloud with a partner, or with the whole room, that helps them to be committed to following-through. I also sometimes offer delegates on our training courses the option of a further conversation about a month after the event to help support this follow-through.

Feedback

There are several approaches that can be used to collect feedback at the end of an event.

Having each individual in the room provide short feedback on what they have learnt and what they plan to do is one way to do this.

Another approach is to review the original list of expectations and check to what extent people feel they have been addressed.

A quick "After Action Review" can be very effective. I describe this in Chapter 4 as one of the tools for facilitation.

Finally, asking people to fill in some type of event evaluation or feedback form can be very helpful. I typically issue these in paper form for people to fill in before they leave the room – ensuring that I allow enough time to do this. This will ensure that most people complete and return it. However, sending an electronic form for people to return after the event is also an option – albeit with a probable lower rate of return. Either way, you can collate the feedback – anonymously is best – and share this in the form of a report with the client. An example of a feedback form is included at the end of this workbook.

Individual or team exercise 3.1 What steps will you take to manage your participants?

We have explored a whole range of approaches for managing participants in this chapter and these are summarized in the following table.

Managing participants	Approaches I would like to try out or adopt	Aspects I would like to focus on
Break out groups and seating arrangements		
Agreeing ground rules		
Clarifying expectations		
Establishing my credibility and building rapport		
Dealing with emotion		
Wrap-up: Reviewing action plans		
Wrap-up: Collecting feedback		
Anything else		

Review the list of approaches to select those that you would particularly like to try out or adopt in your next event(s). Next to each one, make a note of the aspects that you would like to focus on.

You might want to take a photocopy of the completed table and keep it somewhere to hand to use it as an action plan or reminder.

Closing thoughts

There is a lot involved in managing participants in a way that will create a positive and productive environment. It is something that will draw on your emotional intelligence[6], as well as on your organisational skills. These are aspects that you are likely to want to continue learning about and developing.

I have found it particularly beneficial (and restful!) to participate in events as a delegate, and to observe and learn from other facilitators. You might like to explore such opportunities as part of your learning and development too.

Chapter 4. Selecting your Tools

"A facilitator's toolset is a treasure trove to choose from, enjoy and continuously enrich."

Figure 4.1 Selecting tools for facilitation

Background and principles

It was the wide selection of frameworks and tools, and in particular those that I encountered for process improvement, that first drew me to facilitation. There is such a choice of established structures to support different ways of thinking that it is like having a well-stocked box of toys to play with. And of course it is always possible to discover and to invent more tools, and to adapt them to different purposes.

As I have said before, facilitation is all about providing people with the conditions to support their thinking, and the tools for doing so are very much a part of that. Edward de Bono is one of my sources of inspiration for all of this (see for example: *Thinking Course: Powerful tools to transform your thinking*[7]). De Bono works on the principle that we need to develop our skill in thinking, so that we are more conscious of which approaches we are using, how we are using them, and how we could use them more effectively in any given situation.

As De Bono says, selecting the approach you will take, or the tool you will use, is a bit like practising a sport where we might have a choice about which golf club, tennis stroke, or volleyball position to adopt to achieve the desired result.

There are also some basic good practices for facilitation, and some custom ones for the different kinds of events that you might facilitate. Each of my previous workbooks describe the tools for specific situations in some detail, so what I will do in this chapter is first cover basic good practices that I have not described elsewhere. I will then give an overview of the tools for specific situations, referencing my other workbooks, and just select one or two tools each time to cover in more detail.

I will also describe which tools to use for each of the three practical scenarios, and document the approach for these in the form of detailed agendas.

Basic good practices for facilitation

Knowing which hat you are wearing

A facilitator can wear a few different hats during the course of an event – so, echoing De Bono, it is important that you, and the participants know which hat you are wearing, when and why.

Leader vs. facilitator - If your client is in the room, then the chances are they are responsible for leading the event, and you are responsible for supporting them. The person leading the event is accountable for clarity around the goal of the event, the engagement of the participants and the commitment for follow-through from the outcome. They will also have the specialist knowledge about the content to be covered.

Your role, as facilitator, is to ensure that the conditions are as conducive as possible for achieving the desired outcome – that includes everything that we have explored so far in this workbook, along with the choice and use of tools that we are covering in this chapter.

I have found my most productive events to be those where there is close collaboration between the leader and the facilitator. An indicator that this close collaboration is happening is if there is constant and mutual cross-referencing between the two. Topics for discussion could include whether the goals are being met, whether participants are fully engaged, and whether the approach is working effectively.

If either the leader or the facilitator starts working independently at any point and deviates from the planned approach without any kind of consultation, then that is a possible indication of a break down in collaboration.

If the client is not in the room, and you are effectively leading as well as facilitating the event, then you will need to cover the leader's remit as well as you can. The most difficult piece will be ensuring commitment for follow-through. We have discussed possible ways to facilitate that in the previous chapter, under "wrap-up".

Content vs. structure – When I first learnt about facilitation there was a very strong edict that the facilitator should never get involved in the content of discussions. However, that belief got overturned when I participated in workshops led by Dave Hall, of the Ideas Centre[8]. He is adamant that there should always be a clear problem owner in idea generation, and it is their responsibility to choose the solution that will ultimately be adopted. However, he does allow a facilitator to also suggest ideas and solutions, whether they are familiar with the content or not. He takes this approach on the basis that the problem owner will benefit from as much input to his or her thinking as possible.

I now take this more flexible approach too, and participants do generally welcome it. What is important though, as the facilitator, is not to lose track of how the thinking is progressing, and to ensure that a good structure continues to be available (and adapted if necessary) to support it.

Ice breakers

There is a seemingly endless choice of activities to 'warm up' the participants up at the start of an event; to get them at ease with and talking to each other is endless. There are many sources available on this topic[9], so rather than list them all here, I will just refer to some of the ones that we use at RiverRhee.

Introductions. Although people can get very nervous about introducing themselves, introductions are a necessary and invaluable way to build trust and understanding prior to more in-depth conversations during the event.

Approaches we have used include:
- Asking people to use variations on formal introductions:
    - Introduce themselves within their sub-groups only.
    - Introduce themselves to a neighbour, and then have the neighbour introduce them to the rest of the room.
    - Stand up and find someone in the room they don't know to introduce themselves to.
    - Use the 'popcorn' method as opposed to the 'creeping death' i.e. to speak when they feel they want to, rather than following a sequence around the room.
- Giving people some themes to play with:
    - Address specific questions when introducing themselves e.g. their name, where they are from, their role, why they are there.
    - Share something unusual such as 'a little known fact' – like a hobby, or something that has happened in their lives that others may not know about.
    - Share something they are glad, sad or mad (passionate or angry) about. This one is quite good to use as a warm up activity, and to help people centre themselves on a second day for events that last more than one day.

It is a good idea, especially if including something a little unusual in the introductions, for the facilitator to demonstrate the activity first. This helps to ensure that the delegates understand what you want them to do, and also may reassure them that it is 'safe' to do so.

Other ice breaking activities. Activities that get people standing up and moving around have the added advantage of injecting a bit of energy into the day. This is especially helpful if a lot of time has been spent in individual reflection, or in listening to presentations, or in discussions in small sub-groups.

Examples of these kinds of activities include asking participants to:

- Find others in the room who may have the answers to specific questions on various arbitrary subjects that may have nothing to do with the actual event e.g. sports, family, travel etc.
- Line up in ascending or descending order based on the month in which they were born, or the number of years they have been working in the company.
- Select an illustration from a range of cards / postcards that resonates with them, or symbolizes the topic under discussion, and then talk to a colleague (or the group) about why they have chosen it. (I have a collection of postcards that I have collected from my local museum, but you can also buy specially produced sets of cards for these kinds of activities[10].)

Whole group presentations and discussions

The facilitator effectively acts as a role model for the thinking that is to take place during an event. We discussed the importance of setting clear ground rules and expectations in Chapter 2 – and it is important that the facilitator observes these too.

Presentations. It is said that people can only concentrate effectively for 20 minutes at a time. So long presentations with no discussion are not generally a good idea. Having some form of visual aid (with illustrations as well as text) to support anything that is being shared will also help people who have different ways of processing information.

Although slide presentations are a commonly used default, they can create a barrier to effective engagement and dialogue. So it is worth experimenting with different ways of sharing visuals, such as using flip charts and posters.

Engaging participants in the discussion. The facilitator will want to involve and engage all participants as much as possible. This includes making sure that no individual participant dominates the discussion, and that everyone is encouraged and supported to have their say.

Good strategies to use where any individual is showing signs of dominating the discussion are:

- Asking the rest of the group in general for other views or questions.
- Asking specific individuals who have not contributed yet for their thoughts (especially if their body language shows they have something to say).
- Asking the individual to 'hold that thought', especially if they are raising things that will be coming up later.
- Capturing their contribution on a flip chart to show that their contribution has been heard and to enable the conversation to move on.
- Asking the group to have one-to-one discussions with their neighbour, or to split into small groups, and then collecting feedback from all participants.

Using a flip chart or whiteboard – I have found using flip charts or whiteboards to record discussion during an event to be an invaluable support for the thinking process.

I believe it is a mark of respect to record what someone has said in a way that is as close to what they have said as possible. I might summarise their comment rather than write it out in full, but I would try to use their own words as much as possible. I would also check with them that I have correctly represented their meaning.

There are some basic things to get right when recording information on flip charts to aid with legibility and comprehension. Here are some of them:

- Keep the font fairly large and legible
- Use upper and lower case rather than block capitals
- Use a range of colours (but avoid yellow or very pale colours)
- Use bullet points or a mind-map

If there is a lot of discussion to record, or if people need time for individual reflection, ask them to record thoughts on sticky notes. They can then put their notes on the flip chart and group them into common themes.

This brings us onto the subject of 'brainstorming', one that I have already referenced in "The Effective Team's High Performance Workbook", and in "The Effective Team's Operational Excellence Workbook" in the context of Edward de Bono's "Six Thinking Hats"[11].

Brainstorming is a technique that most people will have used at some time or another. Done well, it can be an excellent way to get people generating, exchanging and evaluating ideas. This is known as "divergent" thinking – as opposed to "convergent" thinking when the ideas get evaluated and narrowed down to the final solution.

Done badly, brainstorming can result in a few individuals dominating the discussion, others not participating, narrow (or group) thinking and potentially useful options being missed or dismissed out of hand.

So here are some of my insights on how to make brainstorming exercises more effective:

- <u>Accept all ideas as valid – without prior judgment.</u> This is one of the most common and difficult pitfalls of brainstorming. Individuals will judge their own or others' ideas and dismiss them out of hand. The effect of this can be to discourage participation and stifle further suggestions.

Some of the best ideas will arise out of those that at first glance might seem inappropriate. The rule should be "anything goes", or "every idea is valid and valuable". This is where Edward de Bono's "Six Thinking Hats" works so well: he provides a structure to ensure that the divergent thinking is done productively, before beginning the convergent or evaluative thinking.

- Give people generous but limited time for their thinking. In my experience some of the best ideas are those that come up at the end of a brainstorming session. Effective brainstorming involves breaking down participants' internal barriers about what may or may not be possible, and stimulating their creativity through building on their own and others' ideas.

  Limiting the time for brainstorming also creates a sense of urgency, which can itself energise people to come up with more ideas.

- Include 'naïve' participants within brainstorming groups. It is perhaps more by chance than intention that I have had people participate in brainstorming exercises who have not been closely affiliated to the other members of the group. They have either come from different organisations, or teams, or have simply been doing different work to that under discussion. This has in fact been a stimulant, rather than a barrier to effective idea generation.

  In these situations, the 'owner' of the topic under discussion has to explain it in a way that the 'naïve' participant(s) can understand. This can result in assumptions being surfaced and challenged. 'Naïve' participants are also more likely to come up with suggestions that are 'outside the box' – or that break the 'group think' or paradigms (set ways of thinking) of the rest of the participants.

- Give people the opportunity to reflect individually first, and then share what they have come up with. It is a known fact that Introverts are generally at their most productive when they have the opportunity to reflect about a topic on their own, whereas Extraverts generally process their ideas more effectively through discussion with others.

  This combined approach will therefore allow for both styles of thinking.

- Use sticky notes to capture and collate ideas. Sticky notes are a great way for people to document their thoughts, and to then collect, discuss and collate them.

  Ask participants to write one idea per sticky note and give them good quality thin felt pens to write with as the writing will stand out better than with writing pens. Then ask them to group the ideas into common themes or clusters.

  Again, beware of a few individuals dominating how the ideas are collated, and make sure that everyone has a chance to review and agree on the end result.

- Use aids to creativity. Organisations such as The Ideas Centre specialise in the use of aids such as Lego bricks and paint to stimulate people's thinking. There are also other tools such as SCAMPER[12], or frameworks such as SWOT or PESTLE (Political, Economic, Social, Technical, Legal, Environmental) analyses that I reference in the section on Strategy in Team building and development events below.

Break out groups for discussions and exercises

Break out groups are a great aid to enhancing interaction amongst delegates, which is why they have come up several times in this workbook already. People are more like to engage in active discussion if they are in smaller rather than in larger groups. Five to seven people seems to be the maximum optimum size to ensure that everyone participates. Smaller groups are also viable.

It may be useful to assign, or to ask group members to self-assign roles depending on the nature of the activity that you have asked them to undertake. You might want to ensure that there is a facilitator, and that they understand their role. This role includes encouraging everyone to participate, rather than dominating the discussion themselves! Other roles include those of timekeeper and note-taker.

You will want to ensure that the group has mechanisms for recording their thinking and that they use them well – see the notes above about flip charts, white boards, sticky notes. Another approach I have used is having a paper tablecloth on the table on which to record notes.

I have found it sometimes necessary to pick up and offer the pen to someone in the group to encourage them to begin recording the group's thinking.

It is important to give the breakout group clear instructions – so that they know what questions they need to address, how much time they have, and how you are expecting them to provide feedback from their discussions.

Options for collecting feedback include:

- Asking each group to give a run down of what they have discussed. Beware of this becoming very lengthy and time-consuming.
- Asking one group to give a detailed run-down, and then other groups to cite any additions to or differences from that. Beware of subsequent groups still wanting to give a full account of their discussion.
- Asking each group to cite one different item from their discussion in turn.
- Just asking for general feedback.
- Inviting participants to walk around each others groups to read what others have written and then asking for or picking out a few observations.

The approach you choose will also depend on the intended use of the outcome of the discussions. If, for instance, it will all be documented and shared after the event there may be less need to share it verbally during the event.

If the exercise is one in a sequence of exercises, then it may be more useful to reflect upon and share the final outcome in detail, rather than the outcome of each intermediary step.

Individual or team exercise 4.1 Which basic aspects of facilitation would you like to pay more attention to in your next event?

We have explored quite a number of basic aspects of facilitation in this chapter so far and these are summarized in the following table.

Select those aspects that you would particularly like to try out or adopt and write some notes about what you plan to do.

Take a photocopy of the completed table to keep it to hand.

Aspects of facilitation	Areas I would like to try out or adopt
Knowing which hat you will wear for the event: Leader vs. facilitator Content vs. structure	
Ice breakers: Introductions and other activities	
Whole group (1): Presentations and engaging participants in discussions	
Whole group (2): Using flipcharts and whiteboards	
Whole group (3): Brainstorming	
Break out groups for discussions and exercises	

Team building and development events

Team building and development events usually occur for one of three reasons:
- A new team is starting up and wishes to get important basics in place.
- A mature team has identified some specific gaps or topics that it wishes to address.
- There is a significant change that will affect the team and they wish to prepare for it. (This is discussed further in the Managing Change section below.)

The team leader, their manager, or someone in Human Resources usually triggers the event.

Whether the team is new or more mature, it is likely to benefit from some exploration and further development in three aspects:

1. The team's purpose and goals: its strategy
2. The interpersonal relationships within the team.
3. The work practices of the team: enhancing its performance

"The Effective Team's High Performance Workbook" covers these three topics at some length, so I will only touch on them here.

Strategy development

This is the first of the aspects covered in "The Effective Team's High Performance Workbook". In it I describe how to define the vision, mission and values of a team, and how to start to develop more detailed plans.

It is important for a team leader to share their thinking about these topics. If the rest of the team can be involved in shaping them further, it will help to build their engagement as well as providing some potentially useful perspectives and ideas.

Giving people the opportunity to convey their ideas pictorially (for example on flip charts) as well as verbally will tap into people's different thinking and communication styles, and so is more likely to unleash their creativity.

I have also included SWOT and PESTLE analyses in the high performance workbook. These are tools that would usually be used by more mature teams. They lend themselves well to breakout discussions where a group would simply work through one of the templates and then use it as a basis for further business planning.

I use the SWOT analysis in "The Effective Team's Knowledge Management Workbook" too, as a starting point for shaping a knowledge management strategy.

There is more that can be done on the strategy front. It is a good idea to enlist a facilitator who has expertise in this area if this is something that you would like to explore.

Developing interpersonal relationships within a team

Dr Bruce Tuckman, Dr Meredith Belbin and Daniel Goleman are just three amongst the many business experts who have helped us to understand the importance of healthy interpersonal relationships for a high performing team. Goleman's "Building Blocks for Emotional Intelligence"[6] provide some invaluable insights for this.

Emotional Intelligence supports healthy interpersonal relationships. These in turn support individual, team and organisational wellbeing. They fuel the motivation, enthusiasm and energy for creativity, problem resolution, decision-making and getting the job done!

We recognize that everybody is different. We have different ways of seeing the world, different values and beliefs, different motivations, and different strengths.

Team events that help us to understand and appreciate our differences, and how we can work across them are therefore extremely beneficial.

Personality tools such as MBTI (Myers Briggs Type Indicator), Belbin Team Roles and the many others available that can help us to understand some of our differences are ideal aids to include in team building and development events.

It is important to have experienced practitioners give an overview of the personality tools. This ensures that people fully understand all the different strengths and their value in a team. In addition, the discussion should be non-judgmental and emotionally 'safe'.

There are various ways to help people understand different personality types. The Belbin organisation has a few games that can be purchased, for example, to help illustrate the roles, but I have found that a role-play based on a relevant scenario works really well.

People agree to play a role based on one of their strengths, are given a more detailed description to read about the role, and then stay in character in a kick-off meeting on the chosen scenario. If there are enough people in the room, five or six act out some of the roles, and the others observe. The facilitator, observers, and those who played the roles then compare what they heard and saw.

Similar exercises can be done for other personality tools. The various parent organisations and practitioners who have trained with them are likely to have good examples that can be used.

Enhancing team performance

I have identified a number of working practices over the course of my work with teams that are instrumental to helping them attain high performance. I first listed these in "The Effective Team's High Performance Workbook", and have since expanded this list to 14 elements, and categorized them under three headings.

This list is cited in the RiverRhee blog "Temperature checks or diagnostics for high performance teams[13], and re-produced in this illustration that we also use in RiverRhee's management courses.

Good team practices

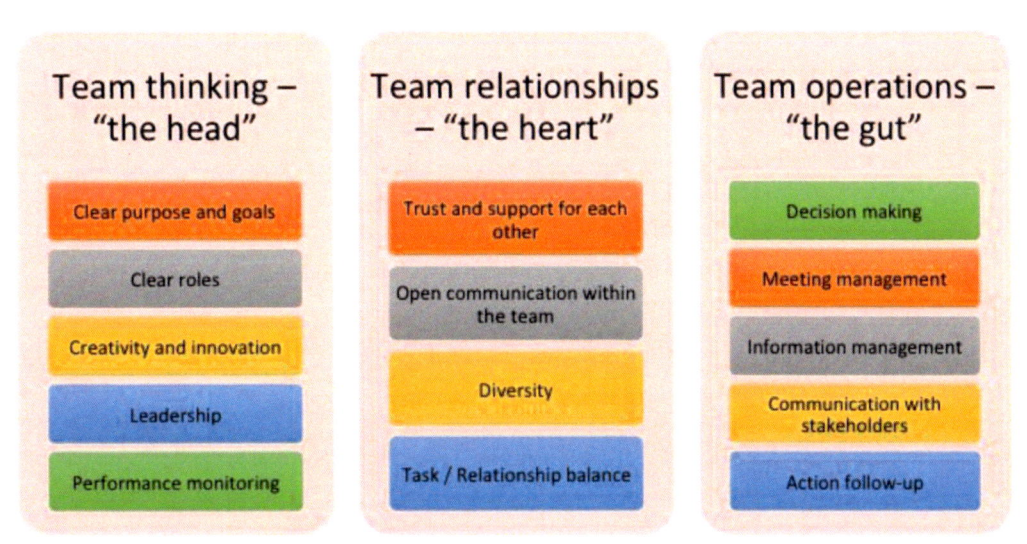

Team thinking – "the head"
- Clear purpose and goals
- Clear roles
- Creativity and innovation
- Leadership
- Performance monitoring

Team relationships – "the heart"
- Trust and support for each other
- Open communication within the team
- Diversity
- Task / Relationship balance

Team operations – "the gut"
- Decision making
- Meeting management
- Information management
- Communication with stakeholders
- Action follow-up

www.riverrhee.com • info@riverrhee.com • tel. +44 (0) 7876 130 817
© Riverrhee Consulting 2017

Figure 4.2 Working practices for high performance teams

I also describe, in the same workbook, how to conduct temperature or health checks, or team diagnostics, to identify what is going well, and opportunities for the team to work together even more effectively.

You will see below that I have planned the team diagnostic as a live exercise during Scenario 1's workshop 2. An alternative is to conduct the diagnostic in advance of the event, either in a series of interviews, or as a questionnaire. The results can then be collated and reviewed with the client ahead of the workshop. They can then presented back to the team at the start of the event. The participants can then just focus on developing their recommendations during the event.

This approach can work well if there is limited time, or if the diagnostic is likely to uncover a lot of potentially contentious opinions. The interview or questionnaire makes it 'safer' for people to give their input, and the results can even be collated anonymously.

The high performance workbook gives more detail about how to construct and use the questionnaire.

Managing change

There is a wealth of frameworks and methodologies for managing change, with an accompanying rich array of tools for facilitating individual and team reflection. My workbook on managing change was the first one I wrote and there have been new developments in the field since then. I do think that the concepts and tools within it are still valid though – and I do still use them with clients.

For those who want something more comprehensive and more up-to-date, you might want to check out the first publication of the Association for Project Management's SIG (Specific Interest Group) on Enabling Change[14]. I was a founding member of this group and co-authored the publication.

I think there are two frameworks that are particularly helpful for anyone dealing with or managing change. The first is to do some self-reflection on your own mindset in relation to a given change. The other is to be aware of the key or common factors for the successful management of any change. I will describe these further and then explore specific approaches for addressing the changes in our practical scenarios.

Mindsets in relation to change

We will all have different perspectives on any given change at work, and it might even be different from one day to another. We may feel very positively towards it, or worried, or even angry. Other things going on in our home lives can also affect our mindsets.

If our task is to facilitate that change, we need to be able to put our own emotions to one side, and develop our awareness of how others are feeling towards it, so that we can help them to work through it as effectively as possible.

Two great tools to build awareness of our own and others' mindsets, and to bring these out in the open are the:

- Positive and negative reaction to change curves, evolved from the work of Elisabeth Kübler-Ross[15]
- "Victim, survivor, navigator" mindsets defined by Richard McKnight[16]

I describe both of these in "The Effective Team's Managing Change Workbook", and have reproduced the illustrations here as a taster or refresher depending on your existing knowledge of these.

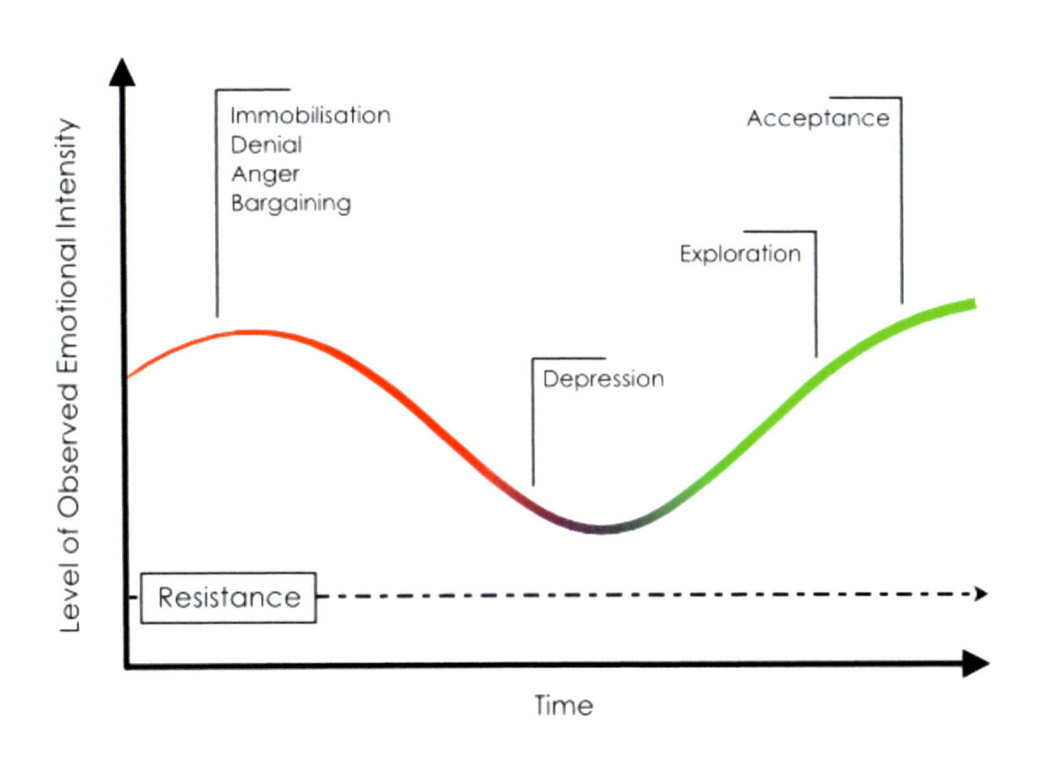

Figure 4.3 Responses to change that are perceived as negative

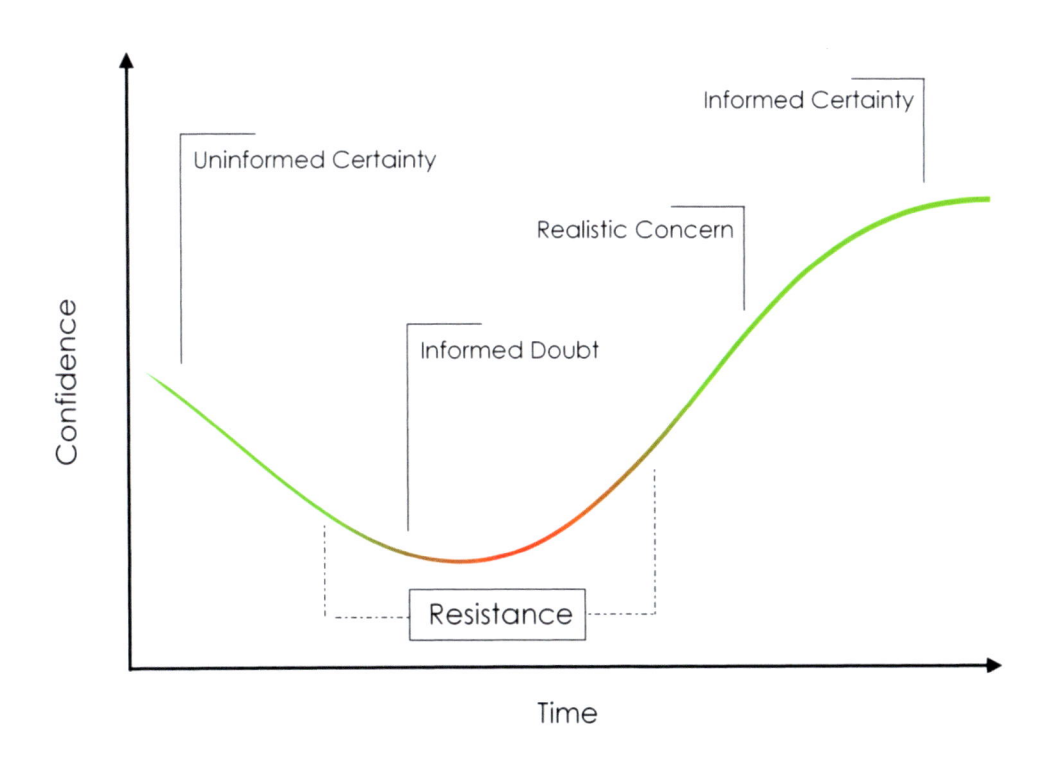

Figure 4.4 Responses to change that are perceived as positive

Figure 4.5 Victim, Survivor and Navigator

Key factors for successful change

Our APM Enabling Change SIG did a lot of testing of what the key factors for successful change might be, in seminars that I led or co-led with our members, and against other existing frameworks. So the following do indeed seem to be the key factors for successful change:

1. Articulate and share a clear vision and strategy for the change, supported by compelling benefits.
2. Ensure that you have strong leadership and visible sponsorship for the change.
3. Define and follow a well-structured approach that is integrated with any existing project management approach in your organisation.
4. Identify all the stakeholders for the change: those who will be affected in some way. Engage with them, understand their perspectives, and gain their commitment and support.
5. Build a strong team to facilitate the change and ensure they have the necessary capabilities for success.
6. Define how you will measure the success of the change initiative. Share the outcomes. Learn from and improve on the results.

Process improvement

In "The Effective Team's Operational Excellence Workbook", I take the reader through Lean and Six Sigma principles and methodology. These can help to streamline existing processes, design new ones, and ensure that the quality of products and services meet customer requirements.

The DMAIC (Define, Measure, Analyse, Improve, Control) framework described in the workbook is ideal for process improvement projects, and there is a vast array of tools to support it.

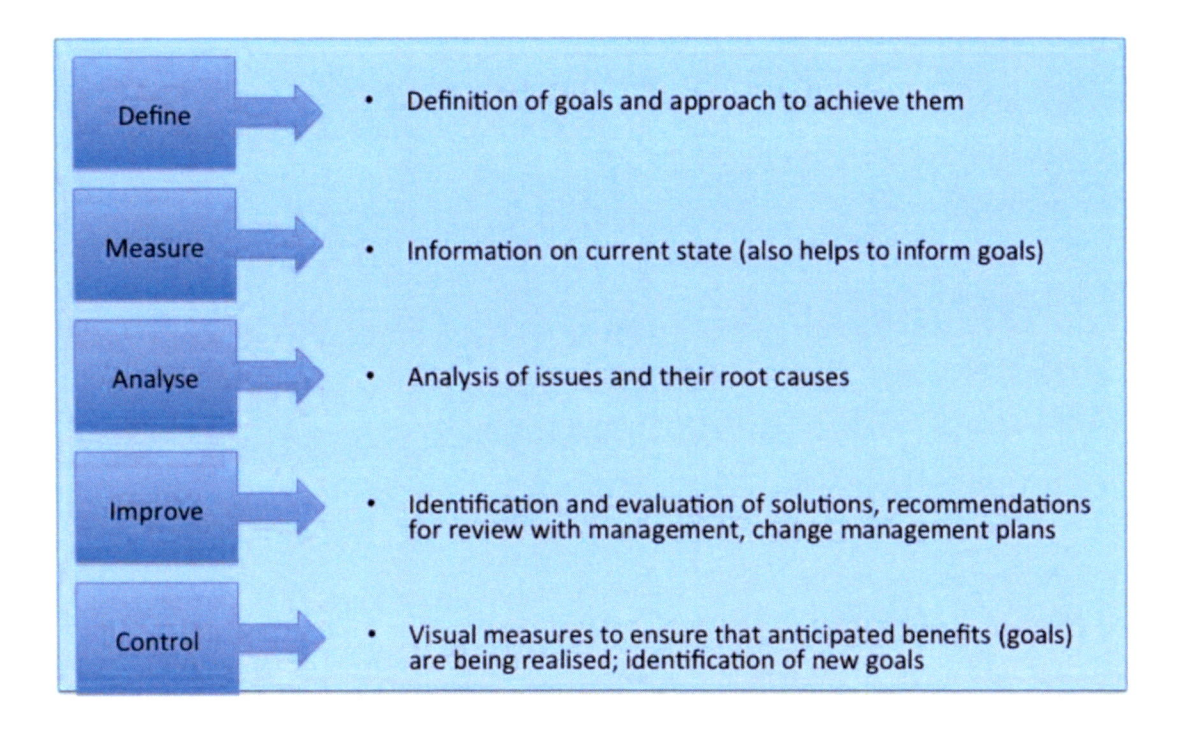

Figure 4.6 Illustration of DMAIC

It is possible to complete a process improvement project within a week if the participants are able to concentrate on it alone, and if they have the support of an experienced facilitator. In practice, process improvement projects are more likely to take a few weeks or months.

It is also perfectly appropriate to use just some of the elements of the DMAIC methodology to suit particular needs. For example, people might map their existing processes, or potential new ones as a pictorial process flow to facilitate discussion and review. This is what I have proposed for Workshop 1 in Scenario 1.

One of the Lean and Six Sigma principles is that those doing the work have the best knowledge to improve it. This principle is congruent with the fourth key factor for successful change about engaging with stakeholders.

Knowledge management

Knowledge management covers many concepts and approaches but chief amongst them are perhaps these four:
1. To encourage people to share and make the best use of what they know in support of organisational goals.
2. To foster conversations as one of the most effective mechanisms for sharing knowledge.
3. To instill learning before, during and after as everyday working practices.
4. To 'codify' knowledge in an organisation's processes and systems so that it can be easily found when needed.

"The Effective Team's Knowledge Management Workbook" takes readers through a methodology for developing a knowledge management strategy and for identifying the tools that will best support them.

The tools that will best support the scenarios covered in this book are those concerned with learning before, during and after. Three of the most commonly learning before, learning during and learning after tools are:

- Peer Assists
- After Action Reviews
- Learning Reviews (sometimes also referred to as Retrospects)

Peer Assists are an intervention for learning from others who have previously done a similar piece of work. When a team is undertaking a new piece of work, it invites those with previous experience to a team meeting so as to get insights on good practices to adopt and pitfalls to avoid.

After Actions Reviews are relatively quick interventions to discuss and learn from a significant activity or event such as a major project milestone. They can also be used at the end of meetings. Typical questions to ask are:

- What was meant to happen?
- What actually happened? (What went well? What could have been improved and how?)
- What can we learn, share, and act upon from this?

Learning Reviews tend to be more in depth versions of After Action Reviews. A facilitator (under the direction of the team leader) will typically issue an initial questionnaire or interview set against a visual timeline of the project's history. Participants are also asked to reflect on what happened: what went well and what could have been improved and how. The facilitator then typically collates the feedback under some common themes ready for review first by the team leader, and then by the participants themselves in a team workshop.

All of these tools and more are described in "The Effective Team's Knowledge Management Workbook".

Scenario 2 uses a Learning Review, and also explores what practices to adopt for learning before, during and after on an on-going basis.

Do note though that even the act of sharing expertise on current and potential processes in Workshop 1 of Scenario 1 is an example knowledge sharing!

Figure 4.7 Learning before, during and after.

Illustrations from the practical scenarios

Each of the scenarios includes one or more of the specialist tools that we have been exploring in this chapter. The full agendas are shown at the end of the book. I have included extracts here where relevant.

Scenario 1 - Running a centralised (shared) business service

This scenario involves significant change for members of the previous teams who are losing some of their responsibilities, but also gaining new ones. There are also important changes associated with starting up the new central team.

We are using workshops in both cases to facilitate the discussion.

Workshop 1

This workshop sets the strategy for the way forward. There are large components for managing the change in remit for the decentralised teams, and to collect their input for developing the new and improved processes.

Strategy:

I started to sketch out the approach for Workshop 1 in Chapter 1. It includes an agenda item where the Head of the group sets the strategic context with a high level overview of the new team's remit.

Managing change:

Participants are given the opportunity to share their perceptions of the change and to start exploring what would help them to embrace it.

In Chapter 3, I talked some more about how this workshop would help them deal with their emotions relating to the change.

Using the change curves as posters for people to reflect upon, and sharing the "victim, survivor, navigator" images will also help with bringing emotions into the open. Participants will be able to develop their own personal strategies for dealing with the change.

The participants will also be better able to support other members of the team having done this reflection on their own responses to the change.

Process improvement:

Team members help to shape the new processes by sharing their experience of good practices and their reflections on what could be improved. This involvement will also help to build their commitment. Here is an extract from the agenda for Workshop 1 relating to process improvement.

Timing	Topic	Approach	Outcome
11:15 – 12:15	Review of processes – Part 1	Break out into 3 pairs to start mapping out 'to be' central processes. Document what works well from current local practices, and opportunities for improvement.	Build on expertise from local library teams in shaping the new processes. Gain buy-in to new processes.
12:15 – 13:00	Review of processes – Part 2	Swap to review one of the other processes and annotate with suggestions / questions as appropriate	
13:00 – 13:30	LUNCH		
13:30 – 14:15	Review of processes – Part 3	Swap to review third process and annotate with suggestions / questions as appropriate	Build on expertise from local library teams in shaping the new processes. Gain buy-in to new processes.

Workshop 2

This workshop focuses on team strategy, interpersonal relationships and team performance for the new central team. It also helps with managing change.

This is how each of these could be tackled.

Strategy:

Timing	Topic	Approach	Outcome
9:45 – 10:45	The team's purpose and goals	High-level overview of the team's remit by Head – with Q&A. Facilitated exercise on Vision, Mission and Values: • Facilitator provides examples of visions, missions and values. • Team members work individually or in pairs (as they prefer) to produce posters (drawings / words) depicting their perspectives. • Walk-about to review posters and identify common elements. • Facilitated group discussion on the key elements to take forward.	Everyone understands the overall intent going forward and has had an opportunity to contribute their perspectives. Agreement on common themes and on actions (who / when) to consolidate them following the meeting.

Interpersonal relationships:

Timing	Topic	Approach	Outcome
11:00 – 12:30	Understanding individual and team strengths and how to use them	Overview of Belbin Team Roles by facilitator. Reflection and discussion around individual and team strengths. Role-play to illustrate and aid understanding of the different team roles in a relevant scenario for the team.	Understanding of individual and team strengths and agreement on individual and team development plans.

Team performance (diagnostic):

Timing	Topic	Approach	Outcome
13:30 – 15:00	Creating strong working practices (Part 1)	Overview of the different working practices by facilitator. Live team diagnostic – rating and Stop / Start / Continue identification of what's going well and what could be even better (done individually with sticky notes on flip charts). Break into self-selecting groups to review outcomes. Participants choose which working practices they wish to review and are asked to write out the recommended action(s) and add their name and a target date for those that they wish to own. Self-organised selection of working practices to focus on to draw out recommendations and individual actions to progress.	Team members engaged in creating a high performance team
15:00 15:15	BREAK		
15:15 – 16:15	Creating strong working practices (Part 2)	Continuation of above. Review and agreement on outputs and next steps.	Agreed actions, ownership and timeframes for creating a high performance team.

Managing change:

Two of the agenda items will help to gain engagement with and commitment for the change.

1. The high level overview of the remit, combined with the facilitated exercise on Vision, Mission and Values
2. The live team diagnostic

These group discussions will help to engage the individuals of the team as navigators for their own change. Both sections also include some tools that could be used to measure the impact of the change.

1. SWOT and PESTLE analyses can be used to inform the strategy at the start, and to make a fresh assessment some time after it has been put in place.
2. Team diagnostics can be used as a baseline for current team performance, and to assess it afresh three or six months down the line.

Scenario 2 – Enhancing the effectiveness of scientific projects

This scenario is a great example of knowledge management, with some implications also for managing change.

Knowledge management:

I described the background and context for this scenario in Chapter 1. The team will be adopting a "learning before, during and after" methodology as an on-going way of working, but would have a kick-off event to set the scene.

This is what the agenda for knowledge management sections of the kick-off meeting could consist of:

Timing	Topic	Approach	Outcome
10:00 – 11:00	Project learning review	Facilitators share a themed summary of the results of the pre-work questionnaire on what worked well and what could have been done differently on a chosen project. Participants are given time to review the detailed feedback in handouts, and on visual displays on the wall.	Everyone hears and understands the feedback from the whole team and knows that their opinions and ideas have been shared. The stage is set for a constructive exploration of the way forward.
11:00 – 11:15	BREAK		
11:15 – 12:30	Identifying potential ways forward for the chosen project	Break into self-selecting groups to review different themes and recommend potential ways forward. Participants choose which themes they wish to review, and are asked to write out the recommended action(s), and add their name and a target date for those which they will own.	Everyone contributing to and owning a part of the way forward.
12:30 – 13:15	LUNCH		
13:15 – 14:00	Review of recommendations for chosen project	Participants feed back their recommendations to the group for review and agreement.	Agreed next steps for chosen project.
14:00 – 14:15	Establishing new working practices for learning before, during and after projects (Part 1)	Facilitators set out some general principles and examples of approaches.	Everyone starts with the same baseline knowledge of potential approaches.
14:15 – 15:15	Establishing new working practices for learning before, during and after projects (Part 2)	Break out discussions (5 groups of 5) on participants previous experiences / good working practices and ideas for a potential way forward. (Reflection on this was also set as pre-work.) Each group shares their recommendations under the 3 headings: learning before, learning during, learning after. Recommendations are consolidated on the spot if the way forward is obvious – otherwise the Team Head and Facilitator take them away for reflection.	Everyone has a chance to contribute.

Managing change:

The participants in this scenario will probably experience fewer emotional repercussions from the changes entailed than those in Scenario 1.

In fact, giving them the opportunity to identify and put in place ideas for enhancing the effectiveness of their projects should engage them and gain their commitment.

In addition, I suggested in Chapter 3 that the team members be asked to reflect about their approach for project management, and to do some pre-work in advance of the workshop. This is reflected in the agenda above. The participants will be better engaged in the changes being discussed through having done this pre-work.

The biggest challenge after that is to ensure that the new ways of working become embedded in their day-to-day project management.

Scenario 3 – Refocusing the approach of an SME (Small or Medium Enterprise)

This scenario has a mix of strategy, interpersonal relationships, knowledge management and some aspects of managing change.

This is how each could be tackled.

Strategy:

The approach here is for the CEO to share their Vision, Mission and Values with just some discussion, rather than active involvement from the team to shape them. This is to set the context for the more important (here) team building, and for the development of the knowledge management strategy.

Timing	Topic	Approach	Outcome
10:00 – 10:45	Strategic overview	Overview from CEO on Vision, Mission and Values, and on opportunities for exploring internal and external knowledge and expertise. (With input from facilitator as appropriate.) Facilitated Q&A.	Everyone engaged and committed to Vision, Mission, Values and opportunities for using knowledge and expertise.

Interpersonal relationships:

Timing	Topic	Approach	Outcome
11:00 – 12:30	Understanding individual and team strengths and how to use them	Overview of Belbin Team Roles by facilitator. Reflection and discussion around individual and team strengths (participants grouped broadly by function). Role-play (by leadership team) to illustrate and aid understanding of the different team roles in a relevant scenario for the team.	Understanding of individual and team strengths and initial ideas for individual and team development plans.

Knowledge management and managing change:

Getting the team members' input to the SWOT analysis and to shape the knowledge management strategy will help to engage them in this change in working practices.

It will also bring in some valuable insights from their experience, expertise, and creative thinking.

Timing	Topic	Approach	Outcome
13:15 – 14:15	SWOT analysis	SWOT analysis in break out groups (6 groups of 5-6 people) to share how well they think the organisation is currently exploiting internal and external knowledge and expertise. (Participants were asked to reflect on this before the workshop.) Suggest mixed teams to help with exchange of ideas across functions.	Everyone engaged in the analysis.

Timing	Topic	Approach	Outcome
14:15 – 15:15	Identifying opportunities going forward	Work in functional teams to draw out ideas for exploiting internal and external knowledge and expertise in the form of a forward plan.	Draft forward plan from each functional group.

Individual or team exercise 4.2 Defining the tools and the approach for your next event

Now that you have read about a range of tools that you might use for different types of events it is time to select your tools and plan your own approach!

Go back to your brief to check on your goals. What kind of event are you trying to organise? What are the broad topics or themes?

What is the facilitator's role going to be? Is there a sponsor or team lead who will also be present? What will their role be?

What are the numbers involved? Will you need to break people into groups? How will you do that? How will you ensure that there is someone in each group, or supporting each group who knows what to do?

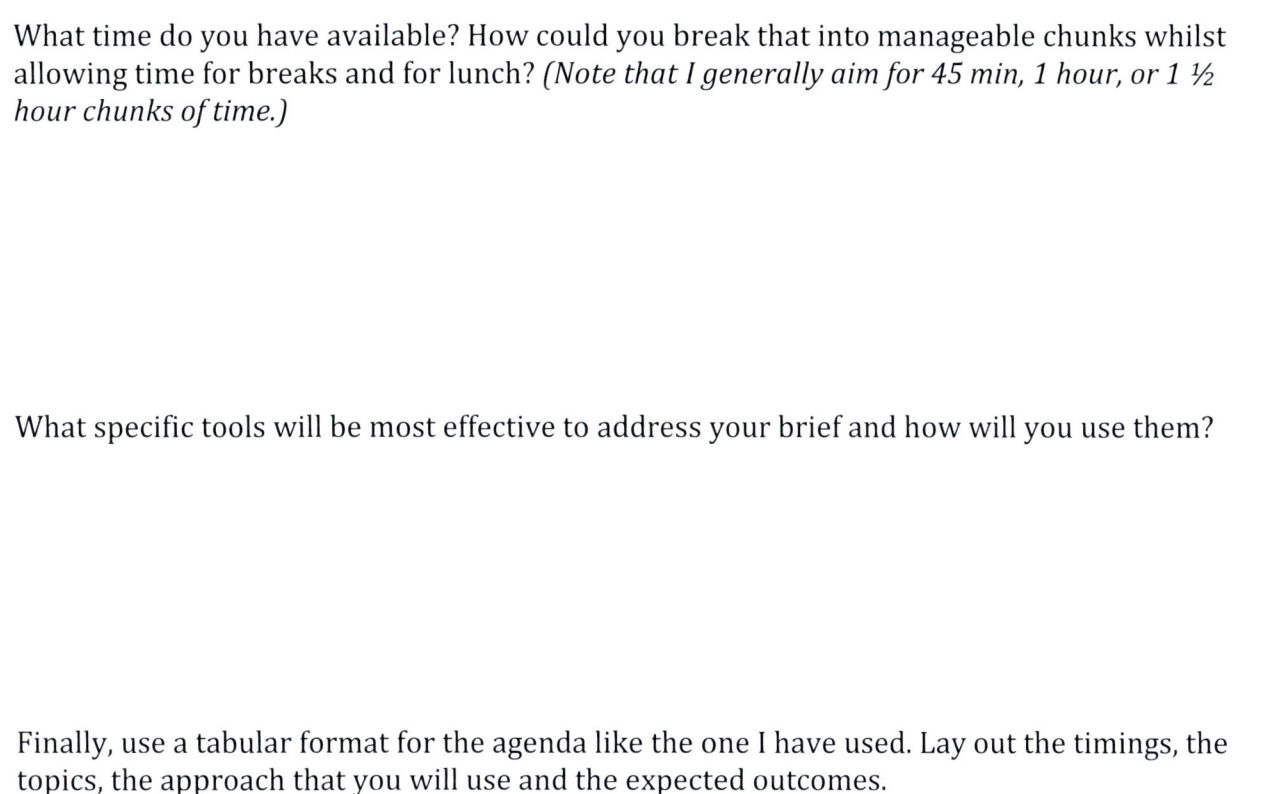

What time do you have available? How could you break that into manageable chunks whilst allowing time for breaks and for lunch? *(Note that I generally aim for 45 min, 1 hour, or 1 ½ hour chunks of time.)*

What specific tools will be most effective to address your brief and how will you use them?

Finally, use a tabular format for the agenda like the one I have used. Lay out the timings, the topics, the approach that you will use and the expected outcomes.

You will also need to make a list of what information (or inputs) and what materials you will need for each session. Some facilitators add this list into their master agenda for the event.

Closing thoughts

Focus groups are another type of event that you might find yourself wanting to set up and facilitate. These are mainly used to design or assess a product, service or feature. Focus group members are often a representative sample of a customer base – for example from different teams or departments in an organisation.

You will need to do very similar things to those we have already explored to ensure that your focus groups are effective. Here are some suggestions:

1. **Clarify the brief** – what is it you want to do, and why? What constraints do you have in terms of time, money and other resources? Who and what do you have available to help you?
2. **Design the approach** – this will include identifying the participants and how you will invite them; making your preparations; ensuring you have the logistics in place; defining the agenda and how you will do things on the day. Focus group meetings can be as short as an hour, or they can last a whole day.
3. **Deliver the event.** Use all of the strategies that we have discussed to ensure optimum engagement and participation.
4. **Follow-up**. It is important to give focus group participants some kind of feedback on the use that you make of their input so that they feel that their time has been well spent. They are more likely to accept a second invitation if that is the case.

People do not usually expect a financial reward for participating in a focus group, but providing a breakfast, lunch or tea will be appreciated. If the participants are from external organisations then it may be appropriate to cover travel expenses.

Agile projects and methodologies have their own framework for facilitated events, which you might already be familiar with, or decide to explore further.

To conclude, I strongly believe in teaching participants in any event to use the tools so that they can continue to use them beyond the event itself.

It is so rewarding when a delegate enthuses about a particular tool and tells me that they plan to go on using it in their everyday work.

At the same time, my approach to using tools is very pragmatic. So I never insist that people should use all of the tools exactly as I suggest. They are there for people to choose from and adapt in a way that works best for them.

Chapter 5. Managing Yourself

"We will be more able to help others be at their best, if we are at our best."

Figure 5. Managing yourself

Background and principles

Facilitation can be extremely rewarding, but it can also be very draining!

We have talked about how good facilitation requires both intellectual skill and emotional intelligence. We need to apply those skills to ourselves so that we can be at our best. If we are at our best, we are more likely to be able to help the people we work with to be at their best too.

As good facilitators we can reflect upon how we are using our various tools, and how we can use them most effectively in different situations.

We can also help ourselves to be at our best by looking after our own emotional and physical wellbeing.

So here are a few hints and tips that might help you to be at your best.

Making the best use of your skillset

Stephen Covey's seventh habit of highly effective people[17] is to "sharpen the saw". If your skill set is all the tools and behaviours that go into facilitation, then these are the ones that you need to continue to "sharpen" to continue to be effective.

There are many ways to develop and perfect your tools. These include:

- Reflecting after individual events on what went well and what you could have done even better
- Asking for feedback from participants, and from co-facilitators
- Observing other facilitators at work, and finding other facilitators to share experiences with
- Reading around the subject
- Attending relevant courses, seminars etc.

Looking after your emotional wellbeing

A facilitator is as much at risk of experiencing the whole pallet of emotional experiences as anyone else. Facilitating a whole day event can be a very exposed and intense experience. It is not unusual to feel such emotions as self-doubt, insecurity, anxiety, frustration, as well as amusement, joy, confidence and pride.

Daniel Goleman et al's "The Building Blocks of Emotional Intelligence"[6] is a great resource for learning about ways to manage your emotional wellbeing. For example, the first booklet in the series focuses on emotional self-awareness. The second one is on emotional self-control.

Emotional self-awareness rests on the ability to detect what we are feeling and how that might be affecting our performance. Emotional self-control is then the ability to regulate how we are feeling and responding to a particular situation so that we can perform at our best.

There is a very strong link between emotions and what is happening in our bodies: our heart rate, breathing and muscular tension. We can learn to tune into these internal signals better. This is known as 'interoception'.

If we can tune into what we are feeling in the moment, we can then learn to better regulate how we are responding to a given situation in the moment.

Here are a few techniques that I have applied and that you might like to try and add to.

Before an event

- Prepare your mind-set so that you feel as prepared, positive and also receptive to the experience as possible. There are various mindfulness, meditation and cognitive behaviour techniques that can help with this – and a wide range of sources available to learn more about these.
- Ensure that you are comfortable with your physical appearance (e.g. clothes, hair) and that this is suitable for the occasion.
- Generally take care of your physical wellbeing (see next section).

During the event

- Consciously adjust (slow, deepen) your breathing – to calm down or stay calm.
- Stand up (or sit down), walk around, stand up straighter with legs slightly apart – to feel more confident.
- Ask someone else (a co-facilitator or a participant) to take the notes on a flip chart – to take the attention off you and give you some thinking time.
- Turn the question back to the audience – to take the pressure off you.
- Introduce a break or a break out activity.
- Have a co-facilitator, participant or leader of the event that you can check-in with – for positive feedback, to consult with, or to alert you to something that you need to be aware of.

After the event

- Give yourself time to unwind and to reflect upon the event, and to celebrate!

As with any area of skill, you can increase your emotional self-awareness through reflection, and through feedback from others. Keeping a daily journal can be one way to help with reflection.

And you can ask a trusted colleague to be alert to and to give you feedback in the moment in instances when you are at your best, or when you are demonstrating types of behaviour that you would like to guard against.

Looking after your physical wellbeing

It can be easy to forget the physical side of things in the intensity of the intellectual and emotional aspects of facilitation. But of course our minds and bodies are inextricably linked.

Pay attention to the following:

- Drink enough water.
- Moderate your intake of caffeine and sugary food.
- Have enough food. (Try to have fresh fruit and / or vegetables.)
- Take breaks.
- Get some fresh air.
- Avoid spending too much time on your feet.
- Avoid getting too warm or too cold.

Individual or team exercise 5.1 – develop your own self-management strategy

What strategies have you, are you already adopting to take care of your emotional and physical wellbeing, and to "sharpen your saw"?

What challenges do you have, or what things are getting in the way of you being at your best as a facilitator?

What new strategies will you try, or what existing strategies will you work on to enhance your self-management?

Closing thoughts

You should now be well equipped to be a good facilitator, and excited about applying some of your new knowledge and skills to your next event.

Remember that, as with all new knowledge and continuing endeavours, not everything will work well or come together at once.

Be patient with yourself and, above all, reflect upon and learn from your experiences.

Listen to others, and then make your own assessment about the best way forward.

Chapter 6. What Happens Next?

"Without follow-through our best intentions will just be idle talk!"

Background and principles

You have now worked through everything that you should need to help the teams that you work with perform at their best. You may have found many things that you would like to think about and implement, or just a few.

As with all new learning, it is important to make an immediate start on applying it, and to keep practising to improve your skills. If you don't do either of these, then your learning will be lost.

Individual or team exercise 6.1 – identify your next steps for taking things forward

Review your notes on the exercises from the previous chapters. What are the top one, two or three new insights that you would like to remember and / or actions that you would like to take forward?

1.

2.

3.

It may be enough that you have written these insights and actions down for you to commit to following-through on them. For some people, having a buddy is an even better way of holding them to a course of action.

How will you ensure that you follow-through on your plans?

Concluding thoughts

This book completes the series of "The Effective Team's… Workbook".

Each book has covered a specialist area for enhancing team effectiveness. As I said at the start of this book, facilitators will often develop expertise in one or more such areas.

Each of the practical scenarios also illustrated one or more of these specialist areas.

Here are the details of the other books for effective teams.

"The Effective Team's Change Management Workbook" (2013) ISBN 978-0-9926323-5-9

This will help you to appreciate personal journeys, reactions and resistance to change and the processes to use when planning and implementing various types of change.

"The Effective Team's High Performance Workbook" (2014) ISBN 978-0-9926323-6-6

This will help you to explore the team development journey, tools for valuing the individual, defining the team's purpose and goals, self-evaluation of the team, and developing good working practices.

"The effective Team's Operational Excellence Workbook" (2015) ISBN 978-0-9926323-7-3

This will take you through a systematic approach for defining and improving how your team spends its time and resources, by ensuring that you are focusing on the right priorities to deliver value to your customers, and that your processes are simplified and streamlined.

"The Effective Team's Knowledge Management Workbook" (2016) ISBN 978-0-9926323-8-0
This will help you to make knowledge management a way of working within your team and organisation. It will explore how organisations can use individual knowledge and expertise, and support learning from others, to make the best decisions, to innovate and to continuously improve.

I would be very interested to hear of any feedback or questions that you may have on any aspect of enhancing team effectiveness.

Please get in touch at publishing@riverrhee.com

Materials for Use in Workshops

Examples of pre-work questions for different situations

1. Documenting processes that the workshop will focus on
(The Appendix mentioned is not included here)

Identify an important and/or frequently used process or procedure that you use in your work that you could use as a case study during the course with a view to identifying and implementing potential improvements to it.

When you select the procedure or process make sure that:

- You are directly involved in this process.
- It is **not** one that you have already been reviewing / improving.
- It is **not** too simple or too complex to work on

Collect two or more of the following items of information for that process or procedure:

i. An SOP or equivalent

ii. A drawing of the layout of the working area (this is likely to be most relevant for a laboratory or other process that involves physical work)

iii. A list of all the people involved if the process is more 'virtual' than physical (this is more likely for an office based process)

iv. An idea of the timelines for the individual steps involved in the process

[Some examples of items ii and iv included in the Appendix to help you.]

2. Initial ideas about what your role could or should be (for a new team)

Clarifying individual roles and responsibilities. [Name] will be briefing us on the overall company objectives. I will facilitate the team through an exercise to define your team goals and how this would be reflected in your individual roles and responsibilities. You will also as a team be agreeing your approach for managing and reviewing objectives through the year, and on a future annual basis.

What you need to do to prepare (to bring to the workshop): Think about what you have been doing within the team so far, your strengths and the things that you care about. How could this be turned into a more formal role description for you, and into a set of objectives that you would want to complete in 2019-20? How would you prioritise your on-going responsibilities and your short –term objectives? Don't worry about word-smithing these at the moment. That will be something to do after the workshop. Please bring your ideas with you.

3. The different working practices important to a high performing team (for an existing team)

Creating strong working practices. I will be facilitating a team diagnostic against various aspects of team working practices (meetings, information management, decision making, continuous improvement etc.) so that you can identify opportunities for improvement and agree approaches for taking these forward.

What you need to do to prepare (to bring to the workshop): Think about the following aspects of team working and how well you feel you are performing them as a team. I will be asking you to score them on a scale of 1-5, where 1 is low and 5 is high.

It will be especially useful to explore any differences in perception, so please keep your views to yourselves for the moment. I will also be asking you to identify what is working well with each of these (and you should therefore continue doing), what you could start doing to make these even better, and what you should definitely not be doing (what you should stop doing).

The aspects of team working are: meeting management, decision making, managing your team's information, following-up on actions, communicating with key people outside of your team (other colleagues at work, customers, "suppliers" etc.). Again, these are your prior reflections to bring to the workshop.

4. Ideas for sharing knowledge (learning before, during and after projects)

Creating a culture of sharing your insights, learnings and expertise about your projects. I will be facilitating discussions at your upcoming team event on how you could more effectively share what you know before you start a project, at key points during the project, and when a project is completed.

What you need to do to prepare (to bring to the workshop): Think about examples of how you are already sharing your insights, learnings and expertise about your projects, and how you could do so even better. If you can also think of the difference such examples have made to the progress of a project, or what benefits you might have gained with an improved sharing of knowledge – bring this information too.

5. SWOT on sharing internal and external knowledge

SWOT analysis (Strengths, Weaknesses, Opportunities and Threats) for sharing internal and external knowledge. I will be facilitating a discussion at your upcoming team event on how you could more effectively share internal and external knowledge.

What you need to do to prepare (to bring to the workshop): Draw out a 4-box matrix on a sheet of A4 paper, labeling the top two boxes as Strengths, and Weaknesses, and the bottom two as Opportunities and Threats.

Fill out each of the four boxes as follows and bring this information with you to the workshop:

- Strengths – these are all of the ways in which you are currently sharing internal or external knowledge well.
- Weaknesses – these are all of the ways in which you are currently not sharing internal or external knowledge well.
- Opportunities – these are opportunities you can think of in which you could share internal or external knowledge well; and ways that might help you to do so.
- Threats – these are potential barriers to you being able to share internal or external knowledge: things that might prevent you doing so.

Feedback forms – an example

[Title of event]
[Date of event]

Name:

Your name: *(Your feedback will remain confidential and will only be used by RiverRhee Consulting in the development of our services.)*

RiverRhee Consulting is constantly striving to be the best that they can be. In order to ensure this happens we invite you to complete this short feedback form.

Please rate each service area on a scale of 1-5, where 1 is unsatisfactory and 5 is excellent

Service	1	2	3	4	5
1. Quality of presentations					
2. Interactive exercises and discussion					
3. Overall ambiance					
4. Quality of handouts					
5. Overall value of the event					
6. Extent to which the event met your expectations					
7. Extent to which you would recommend RiverRhee Consulting to others					

Please comment:

8. What did you find of greatest value in the event?	9. What are your next steps as a result of this event?	10. If you were to attend another event of this type in 6-12 months' time, what do you think this should address?

Please add any further comments here

Thank you!

55

Fully Developed Practical Scenarios

The following are the consolidated notes for each of the three scenarios, taken from the various chapters of this book.

Scenario 1: Running a centralised (shared) business service

Background and context (Chapter 1)

The central library is picking up responsibility for core processes such as purchase of print and electronic resources, subscriptions and loans. It will support and be linked to a network of local libraries that interface with local business (or functional) groups. The head of the new central library has asked for two facilitated events:

1. A workshop with representatives from the local libraries to:
   - Prepare the representatives for the change in responsibilities between the libraries
   - Agree the remits of the central and local libraries
   - Gain the representatives' input to shape the new processes that will be put in place.

This is to be a one-day event, led by the head of the central library, and attended by the team leaders of each of the five local libraries. It will be held in the main meeting room of the central library and will be facilitated by an external facilitator.

2. A start up team building event for the new central library team. This is to take place three months after the first workshop, once the members of the team have all been recruited. The purpose of this event will be:
   - To define the vision, mission, values of the group
   - To clarify roles, responsibilities and priorities for the next few months
   - To help the team understand its strengths and to start building strong relationships within the team
   - To agree working practices for the team

This will also be a one-day event, led by the head of the central library. It is anticipated that there will be three additional team members. The event will also be held in the main meeting room of the central library, and will be facilitated by an external facilitator.

The approach - Workshop 1

Timing	Topic	Approach	Outcome
9:30 – 10:00	Welcome and introduction	Opening words from Head and Facilitator on goals and approach for the day. Introductions from team leaders on their expectations from the day.	Everyone aligned on goals, approach and expectations from the day.
10:00 – 11:00	Introducing the new remits	High-level overview of the new remits by Head – with Q&A. Facilitated exercise on perceptions of the change and what would help people to embrace it.	Everyone understands the overall intent going forward and has had an opportunity to air opinions and feelings relating to it. Head and individuals understand what they can do to help move forward positively with the change.
11:00 – 11:15	BREAK		
11:15 – 12:15	Review of processes – Part 1	Break out into 3 pairs to start mapping out 'to be' central processes. Document what works well from current local practices, and opportunities for improvement.	Build on expertise from local library teams in shaping the new processes. Gain buy-in to new processes.
12:15 – 13:00	Review of processes – Part 2	Swap to review one of the other processes and annotate with suggestions / questions as appropriate.	
13:00 – 13:30	LUNCH		
13:30 – 14:15	Review of processes – Part 3	Swap to review third process and annotate with suggestions / questions as appropriate.	Build on expertise from local library teams in shaping the new processes. Gain buy-in to new processes.
14:15 – 15:15	Review of new remits	Facilitated discussion to agree: 1. Next steps to flesh out new processes. 2. Further clarifications and any actions needed for remaining clarification of new remits. 3. Extent to which discussions have addressed concerns / actions needed for change.	Clarification of new remits and of remaining next steps for embracing the change.
15:15 – 16:00	Wrap-up	Facilitated review of all actions – who is going to do what / when. Documenting of individual action plans. Feedback on the session.	Agreement on responsibilities and timings for action. Feedback on the day and how future sessions could be conducted.

Workshop 2.

Timing	Topic	Approach	Outcome
9:30 – 9:45	Welcome and introduction	Opening words from Head and Facilitator on goals and approach for the day.	Everyone aligned on goals, approach and expectations for the day.
9:45 – 10:45	The team's purpose and goals	High-level overview of the team's remit by Head – with Q&A. Facilitated exercise on Vision, Mission and Values: • Facilitator provides examples of visions, missions and values. • Team members work individually or in pairs (as they prefer) to produce posters (drawings / words) depicting their perspectives. • Walk-about to review posters and identify common elements. Facilitated group discussion on the key elements to take forward.	Everyone understands the overall intent going forward and has had an opportunity to contribute their perspectives. Agreement on common themes and on action (who / when) to consolidate them following the meeting.
10:45 – 11:00	BREAK		
11:00 – 12:30	Understanding individual and team strengths and how to use them	Overview of Belbin Team Roles by facilitator. Reflection and discussion around individual and team strengths. Role play to illustrate and aid understanding of the different team roles in a relevant scenario for the team.	Understanding of individual and team strengths and agreement on individual and team development plans.
12:30 – 13:30	LUNCH (including time for individual Belbin consultation)		
13:30 – 15:00	Creating strong working practices (Part 1)	Overview of the different working practices by facilitator Live team diagnostic – rating and Stop / Start / Continue identification of what's going well and what could be even better (done individually with sticky notes on flip charts). Break into self-selecting groups to review outcomes. Participants choose which working practices they wish to review and are asked to write out the recommended action(s) and add their name and a target date for those that they wish to own. Self-organised selection of working practices to focus on to draw out recommendations and individual actions to progress.	Team members engaged in creating a high performance team.
15:00 15:15	BREAK		

| 15:15 – 16:15 | Creating strong working practices (Part 2) | Continuation of above. Review and agreement on outputs and next steps. | Agreed actions, ownership and time-frames for creating a high performance team. |
| 16:15 – 17:00 | Wrap-up | Review and feedback on the day. | Team energised and committed to next steps. Any improvements for future events of this type noted. |

Scenario 2: Running a centralised (shared) business service

Background and context (Chapter 1)

The Life Science team is interested in regular facilitated events to capture and share what the team has learnt and can learn from and share with others before, during and at the end of projects.

As this implies a number of different styled events, the brief for the first one will therefore be as follows:

- To focus on an agreed recently completed project and use it as a model for how to conduct a learning review at the end of a project
- To agree how the team will share / address the learnings from the agreed project
- To explore how this approach could be extended to other projects, building in the approaches for learning before and during as well as at the end of projects
- To agree how the team will apply these approaches going forward

This is to be a one-day event, led by the team leader, and attended by all twenty-five members of the team. It will be held in a conference room on the research campus and facilitated by two external facilitators.

The approach

Timing	Topic	Approach	Outcome
9:30 – 10:00	Welcome and introduction	Opening words from Team Leader and Facilitators on goals and approach for the day.	Everyone aligned on goals, and approach for the day.
10:00 – 11:00	Project learning review	Facilitators share a themed summary of the results of pre-work questionnaire on what worked well and what could have been done differently on a chosen project. Participants are given time to review the detailed feedback in handouts, and on visual displays on the wall.	Everyone hears and understands the feedback from the whole team and knows that their opinions and ideas have been shared. The stage is set for a constructive exploration of the way forward.
11:00 – 11:15		BREAK	
11:15 – 12:30	Identifying potential ways forward for the chosen project	Break into self-selecting groups to review different themes and recommend potential ways forward. Participants choose which themes they wish to review, and are asked to write out the recommended action(s), and add their name and a target date for those which they will own.	Everyone contributing to and owning a part of the way forward.
12:30 – 13:15		LUNCH	

13:15 – 14:00	Review of recommendations for chosen project	Participants feed back their recommendations to the group for review and agreement.	Agreed next steps for chosen project.
14:00 – 14:15	Establishing new working practices for learning before, during and after projects (Part 1)	Facilitators set out some general principles and examples of approaches.	Everyone starts with the same baseline knowledge of potential approaches.
14:15 – 15:15	Establishing new working practices for learning before, during and after projects (Part 2)	Break out discussions (5 groups of 5) on participants' previous experiences / good working practices and ideas for a potential way forward. (Reflection on this was also set as pre-work.) Each group shares their recommendations under the 3 headings: learning before, learning during, learning after. Recommendations are consolidated on the spot if the way forward is obvious – otherwise the Team Head and Facilitator take them away for reflection.	Everyone has a chance to contribute.
15:15 – 16:00	Wrap-up	Review and feedback on the day.	Feedback on the day and everyone committed to the next steps.

Scenario 3 - Refocusing the approach of an SME (Small or Medium Enterprise)

Background and context

The organisation would like to hold a team development event to explore options for exploiting internal and external knowledge and expertise.

The CEO would like to remind the organisation of the mission, vision and values of the organisation, and share their perspective of the opportunities available for exploring internal and external knowledge and expertise. She would like to then use the event to:

1. Enhance team members' understanding of the strengths that they can each bring to the organisation. We have agreed that the Belbin Team Roles will be particularly useful for this.
2. Have everyone contribute to a SWOT analysis to share how well they think the organisation is currently exploiting internal and external knowledge and expertise.
3. Explore team members' ideas for what further activities they could undertake to better exploit internal and external knowledge and expertise.

This is to be a one-day event, led by the CEO, and attended by all thirty-five members of the team. It will be held in an external venue and facilitated by an external facilitator supported by an internal member of the organisation.

The approach

Timing	Topic	Approach	Outcome
9:30 – 10:00	Welcome and introduction	Opening words from the CEO and Facilitators on goals and approach for the day.	Everyone aligned on goals, and approach for the day.
10:00 – 10:45	Strategic overview	Overview from CEO on Vision, Mission and Values, and on opportunities for exploring internal and external knowledge and expertise. (With input from facilitator as appropriate.) Facilitated Q&A.	Everyone engaged and committed to Vision, Mission, Values and opportunities for using knowledge and expertise.
10:45 – 11:00	BREAK		
11:00 – 12:30	Understanding individual and team strengths and how to use them	Overview of Belbin Team Roles by facilitator. Reflection and discussion around individual and team strengths (participants grouped broadly by function). Role play (by leadership team) to illustrate and aid understanding of the different team roles in a relevant scenario for the team.	Understanding of individual and team strengths and initial ideas for individual and team development plans.
12:30 – 13:30	LUNCH (including time for individual Belbin consultation)		
13:15 – 14:15	SWOT analysis	SWOT analysis in break out groups (6 groups of 5-6 people) to share how well they think the organisation is currently exploiting internal and external knowledge and expertise. (Participants were asked to reflect on this before the workshop.) Suggest mixed teams to help with exchange of ideas across functions.	Everyone engaged in the analysis.
14:15 – 15:15	Identifying opportunities going forward	Work in functional teams to draw out ideas for exploiting internal and external knowledge and expertise in the form of a forward plan.	Draft forward plan from each functional group.
15:15 – 16:00	Wrap-up	Review and feedback on the day.	Feedback on the day and agreement on next steps.

Further Reading

1. Collison, Chris and Parcell, Geoff (2004) *Learning to Fly*. Second Edition. Capston Publishing.
2. Goodman, Elisabeth (2017) *Conversation s'il vous Plaît! How to run a French conversation group*. RiverRhee Publishing.
3. Walker, Caitlin (2014). *From Contempt to Curiosity: Creating the Conditions for Groups to Collaborate Using Clean Language and Systemic Modelling*. Clean Publishing.
4. Tuckman, B. and Jensen, M. (1977) Stages of small group development revisited *in Group and Organizational Studies*, 419-27.
5. Goleman, Daniel et al (2017) 10: Conflict Management, *in Building Blocks of Emotional Intelligence*. Key Step Media.
6. Goleman, Daniel et al (2017) *Building Blocks of Emotional Intelligence*. Key Step Media.
7. De Bono, Edward (2006) *Thinking Course: Powerful Tools to Transform your Thinking*. BBC Active.
8. https://www.ideascentregroup.com (accessed 25th November 2018).
9. Examples of ice breakers - https://www.mindtools.com/pages/article/newLDR_76.htm (accessed 25th November 2018).
10. Express pack – cards for coaching or team development - https://shop.rsvpdesign.co.uk/expresspack (accessed 26th November 2018).
11. De Bono, Edward (2016) *Six Thinking Hats*. Penguin Life.
12. Explanation of SCAMPER - https://www.mindtools.com/pages/article/newCT_02.htm (accessed 25th November 2018).
13. http://riverrhee.com/blog/temperature-checks-or-diagnostics-high-performance-teams (accessed 25th November 2018).
14. APM Knowledge (2017) *Introduction to Managing Change*. Association for Project Management.
15. Kübler-Ross, Elisabeth (1969) *On Death and Dying*. Routledge.
16. McKnight, Richard (2010) *Victim, Survivor or Navigator? Choosing a Response to Workplace Change*. TrueNorth Press.
17. Covey, Stephen R. (1999) *The 7 Habits of Highly Effective People*. Simon and Schuster.